ELFRIDA EDEN FALLOWFIELD

THE
DANCING
debutante

ADVENTURES ON AND OFF THE STAGE

For Michèle,
My dancing Goddaughter,
With much love
from

Effie xx

November 2014

ELFRIDA EDEN FALLOWFIELD

THE
DANCING
debutante

ADVENTURES ON AND OFF THE STAGE

MEREO
CIRENCESTER

Mereo Books

1A The Wool Market Dyer Street Cirencester Gloucestershire GL7 2PR
An imprint of Memoirs Publishing www.mereobooks.com

The Dancing Debutante: 978-1-86151-331-1

First published in Great Britain in 2014
by Mereo Books, an imprint of Memoirs Publishing

Copyright ©2014

The address for Memoirs Publishing Group Limited can be found at
www.memoirspublishing.com

The Memoirs Publishing Group Ltd Reg. No. 7834348

Cover design - Ray Lipscombe

The Memoirs Publishing Group supports both The Forest Stewardship Council® (FSC®) and the PEFC® leading international forest-certification organisations. Our books carrying both the FSC label and the PEFC® and are printed on FSC®-certified paper. FSC® is the only forest-certification scheme supported by the leading environmental organisations including Greenpeace. Our paper procurement policy can be found at
www.memoirspublishing.com/environment

Typeset in 11/15pt Bembo
by Wiltshire Associates Publisher Services Ltd. Printed and bound in Great Britain by Printondemand-Worldwide, Peterborough PE2 6XD

FOR RICHARD

Without whom there would have been no
Timothy, Nicholas or Laura
Or Juliet, Paula or Jamie
Or Caia, India, Hamish, Sebastian or Thomas

With love and gratitude

CONTENTS

Acknowledgements

ACKNOWLEDGEMENTS

I would like to thank all my family for their support, especially my husband Richard, my daughter Laura Eynon, my daughter-in-law Juliet Fallowfield and her daughter India.

Also Liz Rigby, who gave me the courage to continue, and Nicola Willmot for her initial editing and sound advice.

My thanks to Chris Newton of Memoirs Books for all his hard work, unfailing patience and great sense of humour, and to Memoirs' designer, Ray Lipscombe, for his design work on my book.

Also to Vicky Edwards of Elly Donovan PR for all her interest and help and Barry Swaebe for allowing me to use his photographs.

My thanks to friends who have encouraged me, especially Jean Bird, Alexandra Colquhoun and Alison Wheatcroft.

Finally to Mary Stassinopoulos and Lee Williams, who gave me the idea in the first place, and all the pupils and staff who have been associated with the Vacani School of Dancing from 1982 to the present day.

CHAPTER ONE

WAR BABY

"I was born on the day France fell, and I went to France that very day. And do you know? All the houses were lying completely flat on the ground!"

This was what I related to my friends over and over again, as I firmly believed it to be true. It's true that I was born on the day France fell – 17th June 1940. Somehow I got it into my head that my mother and I had taken a train through France, and as I peered out of the window, with my little fingers poking through the holes of my shawl, I had seen serried ranks of houses, all neatly lying on the ground as flat as pancakes!

In reality my poor mother had a horrible time. I can well understand the reluctance of the population to come to terms with the fact that we were in the midst of another world war.

"This one will not last long," everyone agreed. "Nothing could be as bad as the last war, the war to end all wars!"

Tragically they were all proved wrong, and so began the great exodus of children from the cities to safer parts of the country – though in our case, it was to a safer part of the world.

It was decided that my mother and her sisters, with the help of our old nanny, should take the children of certain friends to Canada for the year or so the war was expected to last. The risky business was of course getting there, although they felt confident that the Germans would not attack civilian convoys containing mainly women and children.

My mother, Patricia, Lady Eden, had found a suitable house for rent in Vernon, BC. The timing was not brilliant and as she was about to give birth to me, she opted to stay in London while my Aunts Meme and Phil, with Old Nanny, escorted 12 children to the safety of Canada.

While she was lying in her hospital bed recovering from her third caesarean section operation (quite dangerous in those days), the news came through that the convoy had been attacked by U boats, and that a ship carrying women and children had been sunk. The news was terrible and frightening, and it was not until several days afterwards that my mother heard that it was not 'her' ship that had gone down.

At the age of three weeks I accompanied my mother and the rest of our family on the treacherous voyage to Canada. In all we were sixteen children. Mummy was very weak, and understandably nervous. It must have been dreadful for my father, who had to say goodbye to my sisters, Ann, Rose and Amelia and my brother John, as well as his wife and newborn baby.

According to Mummy, as our ship sailed into the safety of the St Lawrence River, there were huge cheers from the crowds lining the embankments. There too was the rest of our party waiting for us to arrive, before the train journey across Canada could be continued. I am told the journey was long and boring, and when we arrived at our destination, the house that had been rented was in a dreadful condition and almost uninhabitable.

With her sisters in tow, my mother descended on a local hotelier. "Please can you help us?" she pleaded. "We are mothers and children (plus a newly-born baby) who are fleeing the terrors of war torn Europe to the safety of Canada. Unfortunately the house we had hoped to rent is totally unfit for our purposes."

The hotelier was a kind man. He took us all in while the house was cleaned up, and he helped to publicise our plight.

Some months later a man called Colin Breaky contacted my mother and offered us the use of his house in Breakyville (named after him), outside Quebec. Back we all went on the long train journey, although this time at every station there was a welcoming party of people who showered us with presents and food, and even on occasions a band would be playing!

Mummy told me they had to resort to throwing goodies out of the windows as the train slowed before the next station, in order to appear suitably bereft. We never forgot the kindness and generosity of the Canadian people, and I benefited from living in Canada for the first few years of my life.

Chaudière House was a magical place. The exterior was wooden, painted in black and white with beautiful balconies and verandas. There was a huge garden, and thanks to the immense generosity of the owner, Colin Breaky (now Uncle Colin to us all) we had slides, see-saws and swings of all sizes to keep us amused.

During our second year there, Uncle Colin had a little

playhouse made for me. It had two floors, and furniture of pale blue wood with rounded legs. I had my own little kitchen, well fitted out, where I pretended to cook wonderful meals. I would then stand at my front door and imperiously ring the small silver bell with an amethyst in its handle that Uncle Colin had given me, and demand that my elder siblings and cousins should come and eat my imaginary food.

I was not very popular with the other children. I could even go so far as to say they really didn't like me at all. If they wouldn't play I would bawl, and then they would get into trouble. They tried to get their revenge by being beastly to me – only to be usually spotted by one of the adults.

Mummy inevitably spoilt me. She enjoyed being able to look after me all by herself. Uncle Colin was the only father figure I knew. I have no recollection of a surprise visit from Daddy, but he wrote me a charming poem at the time, part of which is as follows:

Ah sweetest child, where will thy lunges and thy gallant
tottering lead thee before thy journeying is done, and thou art
wearied of the sun?
Dear One Year Old, your smile tears at my heart. You play in
this bad world an angel's part.
Go to thy mother, and there upon her breast,
Take, while thou may, thy refuge and thy rest.

Breakyville had been built on the shores of the St Lawrence River. I remember being old enough to accompany all the children to watch the enormous tree trunks colliding and cascading down the river as the loggers, with incredible nimbleness and balance, leapt from one tree to another to free them from entanglement before sending them hurtling on their way.

During the snowy months of winter, when I was warmly dressed in my little white fur coat and hat with a long, red woollen sash tied round my tummy Canadian-style, Uncle Colin would take us out on horse-drawn sleighs to see the maple syrup being extracted from the trees. Then – best of all – we were given little paddle sticks with which to scoop up the syrup from tables, before dropping some of it on the snow to harden so we could suck this deliciousness slowly to our hearts' content. No one cared about tooth decay or cholesterol in those happy days!

The one year became two, and then stretched to three. Still the war continued. Families were becoming restless and wanting to see their children again. The older children all went to schools in Canada, while my mother taught the younger ones at Chaudière House. She did quite well, and the children learned the basic school subjects as well as dancing. Mummy even produced a charming production of *Peter And The Wolf.*

My mother also had a clinic for babies and toddlers. It all began when she saw a puny baby when she was taking me for a walk in my pram and persuaded the baby's mother to let her have her daughter for a few days. In no time at all, under her guidance, the baby thrived. From then on the word spread, and mothers would line up outside the gates demanding help for their children. In the end Mummy was looking after about 30 babies, with the help of Meme and "Old Old" Nanny. Unfortunately she did go a bit too far, as she encouraged the women to use some sort of birth control. The local Roman Catholic priest descended on her in fury, and my mother had to promise never to do such a dreadful thing again.

It must have been with a heavy heart that my mother bowed to pressure from the parents of the children she was caring for to return to Europe. We were safe and happy and well fed where we were, and no one knew what to expect once we were home again.

In 1943 we sailed in a neutral Portuguese ship from New York to Lisbon. While I have no memories of the voyage, my stay in Lisbon is firmly imprinted on my mind because Mummy always insisted I had an afternoon rest. I was put to bed in a darkened room in the hotel where we were staying, and Mummy even took the bulb out of the bedside lamp to ensure I would stay in total darkness. After she had left the room and my eyes were accustomed to the gloom, I curiously wondered how on earth light could come out of a lamp. Naturally I stuck my fingers inside the socket, and turned on the switch.

I think my screams could have been heard in Canada. "A duck has bitten me!" I cried. Meanwhile my mother could not get in, as the door was self-locking. She too was screaming, but at last the door was opened and I was being comforted in her arms.

I was aware of an underlying sensation of nerves and tension as we waited in our hotel for a flight to take us home to England – "We're going today – no we're not – maybe tomorrow – quick, hurry, we're going now!" I was bundled up in a blanket and there we were amongst a group of people, hurriedly climbing on board an aeroplane which was lower at the back than the front. It was dark, and although my mother and I were at the back, I knew the plane was as full as it could be.

"Hurry everyone – sit down – we're leaving" we heard, and the plane slowly started to move. But the door was still open! Suddenly someone was running alongside the plane and my mother let me go and leapt up to help. "Here" she said, "Take my hand." I was screaming, as I thought she was going to fall out of the aeroplane. Others came to her aid, and between them they hauled the man inside and closed the door, seemingly seconds before we were airborne.

It was crazy, really, to leave the blissful haven of Canada for the dangers of London. I can't imagine what 'they' were thinking of!

We returned to the beautiful flat we owned in Albert Hall Mansions, right beside the Albert Hall. I had a lovely new Nanny, Nellie Packard, who would take me for walks in Kensington Gardens in a big old-fashioned pram (a pram, even though I was three years old), and I would amuse her by asking to go by the Albert ME-morial to look at all the animals carved round its perimeter. I was also fascinated by the many 'garage' balloons I saw suspended in the air. How strange, I thought, for people to put their cars in balloons and then float them up in the air! I was unaware that these barrage balloons were there to act as a deterrent against low-flying enemy aircraft.

One day my mother took me for a walk in the park while Nanny was out. She was tired and sat on a bench, but kept her eye on me as I became engaged in a deep conversation with a poor-looking man who had with him three scruffy children. Eventually this man came over to my mother and politely told her that I had been upset at the state of his children's clothes and had told him that I had masses of clothes at home I never wore and that he should come and help himself.

My mother found herself in a difficult position. I did not, apparently, have masses of clothes, although I was certainly well dressed. Anyway, the father and children came home and my mother duly handed over nearly all my clothes for both day and night. Nanny came back the next day and was furious. Clothes were strictly rationed and we had no more coupons to buy anything new, and I didn't even own a spare vest or a pair of panties. Nanny rang round all her friends and managed to beg and borrow some coupons, so at least I had something to wear.

One evening that October, when I was four, I had apparently been naughty about going to bed. Again Nanny was not there, and my mother at last got me to sleep in my little bedroom overlooking the park. Deeply asleep, I was dimly aware of being lifted up by my mother and taken down the huge staircase, where with my sisters, cousins and Aunt Meme I sat on a chair placed under the banisters. Outside we could hear the wail of the sirens, and the air was filled with anticipation and what I later realised was fear.

The telephone rang on the other side of the hall and my mother went to answer it. After talking briefly she said, "Hello? Hello? Oh we've been cut off." Then she came over to us, and as she did she said, "That was Daddy" (he was working in the War Office) "and he said we should get into the shelter immediately as the raid is in our area."

No sooner had my mother said that than we heard the sound of what I assumed to be an aircraft over our heads. We sat as still as statues. Then there was an ominous silence almost immediately, followed by a huge cacophony of noise. There was dust and debris everywhere, but we were still sitting under the banisters facing the enormous double front doors of the flat. As we sat in total shock, these doors, as if in slow motion, detached themselves from their hinges and fell in unison towards us. They landed on the banisters, with all of us safely beneath them.

Suddenly we heard another drone and realised this was a second flying bomb, or 'doodlebug' as they came to be called.

Once again the engine cut out seemingly right over our heads. We were sitting under the huge doors as we waited for the inevitable explosion, only this time it did not come. Nothing happened.

We decided to find our way to the shelter, picking our way over piles of debris in the main hall and seeing our fellow residents, some bleeding from cuts made by shards of glass, coming down the staircase from the flats above. An elderly lady bleeding from a head wound was carrying her canary in a cage.

In the shelter there was a maid, complete in uniform of black dress and white pinafore and cap, sweeping the detritus from the floor as if it was the most normal thing in the world. The shelter was in reality a coal bunker, and I was placed on a large shelf. As I sat there my teeth chattered uncontrollably, and I remember saying to my mother, "My teeth are wobbling and they won't stop!" Someone found me a glass of milk and I calmed down.

The whole of my bedroom window had landed on my bed, slicing it in half. My mother was endlessly grateful that she had decided to wake me up after all.

The second bomb never did explode. It was defused. If it had, it would have wiped us all out. My mother kept a bit of 'our' bomb as a souvenir, which I now show my grandchildren as I regale them with my 'bombed out' story.

CHAPTER TWO

RETREAT TO THE COUNTRY

We were the lucky ones; we had another house we could go to. This was in the New Forest, in a village called Fritham. The house itself, a large glorified villa, is still standing, but nowadays it is a nursing home. I grew up in it, and loved it, but I can see today that it was rather an ugly house. It had nine bedrooms, most of which were very large, and three attic rooms. There were four bathrooms. The house had a large annexe and three cottages, a farm and large kitchen garden. In all we had just over twenty acres, which was small fry in comparison to Windlestone Hall, which had been the Eden family home.

From the upstairs windows of the main house one could

look across the trees to Southampton Docks, where the funnels of the great ocean liners would be illuminated at night. Unfortunately during this time, we also had a good view of Southampton burning, as this city was also a main target of the German bombers.

During the raids on Southampton, we would either all sleep in the passages between the bedrooms, or if the raid seemed really near, we would go to the shelter which had been dug into our field. I *hated* going to the shelter. It was dark, dank and smelly. There was a constant rustle of animals, probably rats, and there was nothing to do but sit with our feet curled under our bodies, clutching our gas masks and waiting for the planes to disappear.

During the war there were many airfields in the New Forest. Being on the south coast we were conveniently close to France and the Channel Islands. One of these airfields was at Fritham, and this was occupied by the Americans. My elder sisters and cousins were in their element! These gorgeous Americans with their wonderful accents were more than friendly, and happily handed out bars of Hershey's chocolate, which were like nectar for us in our strictly sweet-rationed world.

Once in a while the aerodrome was opened up for visitors. I remember going with Nanny and climbing up into a plane while an American told us about the war. I was bored at this, but it was worth it, as we were then allowed to slide down a rope from the cockpit.

Looking into a hangar I saw a huge round metal object. "Is that a bomb?" I tentatively asked. "It sure is, young lady" replied an American airman, and with that he picked me up and sat me on top of it. I felt the cool metal against my bare legs. I touched it with my hands. "I wonder," I thought to myself, "Will it explode if I kick it?" Not being a child to ask first, I duly kicked it, and thankfully, it didn't explode!

A small bi-plane taxied by. "Are you going up to the sky?" I was able to ask the pilot, who was casually leaning out of the cockpit window. "Sure am," he replied, "Would you like me to get you a star?"

Wide-eyed I watched the plane disappear into the sky, and not long afterwards it reappeared and landed just before us. The pilot jumped out and came to me clutching a small silver star in his hand. I was overjoyed, and totally believed he had snatched it from the heavens for me. I have always regretted that in the ensuing years, this charming little memento was lost. I will never forget the pilot, though.

On my mother's dressing table she had placed a beautiful set of frosted-glass bowls and dishes decorated with tiny rosebuds. I loved these pretty objects, which contained her powder puff, cotton wool and so on, so it was not with a sense of mischief that I curiously wondered - if one dropped a glass against a glass, would it still break? Unfortunately I chose this pretty set to discover that yes, indeed, glass did break when dropped against more glass, and I had a smarting behind for a long time afterwards due to my mother venting her anger and sadness upon me. I had quite a few beatings, I'm afraid, but I am glad to say that I am not traumatised as a result, and it has not turned me into a vicious, slap-happy adult.

On another occasion, when I was five, I decided to run a bath (long after I was supposed to be asleep) and into that bath I put everything I could find. In went precious Lux soap flakes, sweet-scented bath oils, a tin of Gumption, shampoo and talcum powder. My misdemeanour was only discovered when water trickled through the ceiling downstairs, as I had been unable to turn off the taps! Everything I had thrown into the bath had been pre-war. This was a cry one heard again and again, as to have something that was pre-war meant that you had something of quality. I seem to remember Mummy was a bit cross then, too!

During the latter part of the war my father let Fritham House to some monks and the family moved into Kings Garn Cottage, which was in another part of the grounds. I was fascinated by these black-cloaked men, and one man in particular, Father John, became my favourite. Our orchard in springtime was filled with a mass of daffodils, and almost every day I picked a bunch and wandered over to the house to find Father John and present him with my offering. Finally, very tactfully, I was asked to cease this activity, but I still tried to spy on him from our side of the hedge.

VE Day (Victory in Europe) came at last and my cousin Jimmy climbed up to the roof of our house to fix the Union flag (which we all called the Union Jack) onto the spire, which he could only do by using the dog's collar. We all ran through the gardens shouting "VE Day! VE Day!" I too shouted as loudly as I could. Although I hadn't a clue what it meant, I knew this was an incredibly significant and exciting day.

* * *

Poor long-suffering Nanny had her patience put to the test when my mother decided we should keep some goats for milk. Daffodil and Daisy then entered our lives, but no one realised that Daffodil was pregnant. She duly gave birth to Buttercup, and all her milk had to go to feed her baby.

Nanny was pressed upon to milk Daisy. Daisy did not like Nanny, and took every opportunity to bite or kick her.

Nanny and I slept in two rooms on the ground floor of the cottage, and a door from these rooms opened onto the garage, which was devoid of cars (we didn't own one) but made a useful storage place. Unfortunately the goats discovered this door when it was left open and thought Nanny's bed was the best place to be. When one of them wet this bed, that was the last straw. "Either those goats go, or I do" said Nanny, and my mother knew when she was beaten. Amelia and I were very sad to see them go. We loved them.

Quite soon after the end of the war my mother crossed the Atlantic in order to see her youngest sister Phil, who had not returned with the rest of the family. Not having much money, she secured a berth on a merchant ship and the captain kindly let her have his cabin. The crossing was frighteningly rough and the captain would enter his cabin and say, "I hope she don't break her back", which unsurprisingly somewhat unnerved my mother.

My eldest aunt, Meme, was living in one of the other cottages, Moor Cottage. Nanny and I moved in with her while Mummy was away. My siblings were all at school or work and Daddy was busy.

One day, after I had got the impression Mummy would be home soon, I heard Meme saying to Nanny, "Queen Mary is stuck on a sandbank". "Goodness! I thought, "Poor old Queen Mary." The Queen's grandmother was still alive then and in my mind I envisaged this poor woman sitting on a beach where she had obviously gone for a picnic, totally incapable of getting up.

The following day it poured with rain. "Is Queen Mary still stuck on a sandbank?" I asked. After the affirmative reply I imagined a large tent would be erected to cover her. "Why don't they pull her off with ropes?" I asked. "They're trying to" I was told, "but she is stuck fast". At last after three days I was informed that Queen Mary was free, and amazingly just before I went to sleep that night my mother rushed into my room and smothered me with hugs and kisses.

Eventually I learned that a kind friend had insisted my mother should return to England in comfort and had duly paid for her passage home on the great Cunard liner the *Queen Mary*, and it was of course this ship that had been stuck on a sandbank outside Cherbourg.

After that my life at Fritham was full of happy memories of a childhood which was amazingly free and unrestricted. We had a large kitchen garden which was presided over by Mr Gee. The greenhouse smelt deliciously of ripe tomatoes. We would sneak among the gooseberry bushes and gorge ourselves on plump, purplish fruit. Along the walls were peaches and figs, and in their season, the strawberries and raspberries grew in abundance.

My father taught me a naughty little riddle:

"Where's Mummy?"

"She's in the kitchen garden."

"What's she doing?"

"She sits among the cabbages and peas!"

Probably because we had stolen too much fruit, my sister and I often had upset stomachs. We were then dosed with California Syrup of Figs. If we were 'off colour' my mother pronounced us 'liverish' and we had Carter's Little Liver Pills. The worst was if we had a headache, when we were given a dreaded grey powder which was tipped into a spoon of jam in order to disguise the taste. It never did. Best of all was to graze a knee, for then we were dabbed with 'Booty Rouge' (Mercurochrome in a deep red bottle).

My sister Amelia and I became great friends despite the seven-year age gap. Most of the time she was great fun to be with as she was a real daredevil. We were very adventurous and totally fearless.

When I grew older, Amelia introduced me to the fun of climbing on roofs. We used to do this all the time, and it was a habit I continued until my twenties. Somehow we never fell off, and surprisingly, we were never found out.

A high wall bordered the stable yard, and on the other side of it the grass had been allowed to grow very long. Amelia and I thought it would be fun to hold the four corners of a sheet and jump from this wall to see if we could parachute. We took a sheet off a bed, and as my mother looked in horror from the cottage window, she saw her two little girls, arms round each other and clutching an enormous sheet, jumping into oblivion! We had landed on the long grass, quite safely, having sadly discovered that our 'parachute' did not work.

After the war had ended the Americans left, and the airfield was abandoned. The aerodrome immediately became the most wonderful play area. Locked-up huts bearing the words "DANGER – HIGH EXPLOSIVES – KEEP OUT!" provided an instant magnet and a challenge. Deep pits dug to hide anti-aircraft guns were perfect for hide-and-seek games. Best of all was a huge mountain of sand, piled up against a high brick wall. We had no idea what it had been used for, but we would clamber up to the top of the wall and then jump out as far as we could, always landing with our legs deeply embedded in the sand. This enjoyable game came to an end when we were seen by a local man who reported to our father that we were playing in a firing range, and there was a good chance there could be unexploded shells hidden in the sand.

My mother said I never should
Play with the gypsies in the wood.
If I did, she would say
"Naughty little girl to disobey!"

Although we often chanted this short rhyme, we loved the gypsies who visited us every year. My mother always bought pegs from the gypsy women, and although we were not allowed outside our garden when they were in the area and our ponies were firmly kept in their stables, somehow I was never frightened of them. Their beautifully-painted caravans were works of art, drawn by healthy-looking horses. They never overstayed, and even if villagers complained a few things were missing, we knew these people were real gypsies, and part of our country life in those days.

We had a post office and a shop in our little village. The shop was called Winter's, and old Mr Winter, a larger-than-life man, stood behind the glass-fronted counter in his white overalls, while behind him were shelves of tins and jars and exciting-looking boxes. Huge slabs of butter, margarine, lard and cheese were displayed in the glass counter, and on top of this were jars of humbugs, toffees, pear drops, mints and other sweets from heaven.

I accompanied my mother one day to Winter's and waited patiently while she bought some ham, buttons, sewing thread and cheese. At last I was asked if I would like some sweeties. With great deliberation I chose the few I was allowed, and these were carefully placed in a little brown paper bag which was twisted at the corners.

I thanked Mr Winter, and then heard my mother also thank him, before saying "On account please". We left the shop, and to my amazement, my mother did not pay any money.

"You did not pay!" I said as we walked home.

"No" replied Mummy, "I said 'on account'."

I deeply pondered this strange event in my heart. One could buy whatever one wanted and not have to pay a penny. One simply had to say the magic words, 'on account!' I was a very popular little girl during the following week, as I rounded up all the children in the village and marched them to the shop, where I grandly allowed them to choose whatever sweets they liked. "On account please, Mr Winter" I said, and with the grateful thanks of the children ringing in my ears, I danced home.

The following day I learned the truth about 'on account'. Rather a swizz, I thought.

1947 was one of the worst winters on record. Fritham was cut off from the world for days. At Fritham House we were fortunate, as we generated our own electricity and pumped our own water. Today the old engine house and water tower have been converted to unusual and charming houses.

My mother had planned to take me to London to see my first ballet performance at Covent Garden. I was consumed with excitement, and packed my little pink suitcase in readiness. Sadly the taxi could not get to us. I stood looking out at the white landscape, longing for dear Bill to arrive in his car. Finally, after three days of trying, he made it, and took us to Southampton to catch the train for London.

The ballet was *Coppélia,* and the story was of a beautiful doll created by an old toymaker who sat her on his balcony, where she 'read' a book. A young man fell in love with her and was determined to see her. The end of Act 1 showed him slowly climbing the ladder up to the balcony. As the curtain descended my mother looked at me, and there I was, totally engrossed, 'climbing' the ladder with my hands.

This was my first introduction to the world of ballet, a world which would eventually play such an important part in my life.

CHAPTER THREE

FAMILY MATTERS

"Isn't your mother wonderful? How DOES she do it?" My sisters and I were asked these questions so many times we were in danger of becoming bored.

There is no doubt that in many ways, my mother was, indeed, wonderful. She was also a complex, talented, emotional, loving, demanding and extraordinary woman.

I grew up thinking that my mother had been born Patricia Mary Prendergast. It wasn't until after her death that I discovered she had been christened Edith Mary White. My grandfather was Arthur Samuel White, and he was born in Boston, USA. His mother had been married before and he had a half-sister called Marie Prendergast, who had a beautiful voice. Miss Prendergast, who had changed her name to Marie Halton, became a very well-known 'lieder' singer who found fame in Europe.

Marie decided it would be good for her brother to join her in Europe, and for reasons of simplicity, to use her surname of Prendergast. Arthur agreed, but to remind him of his real identity he was universally known as 'Whitey' thereafter.

Whitey loved Europe, and while there he fell in love with a pretty young Austrian woman called Rosa, whom he duly married. This marriage produced three daughters called Mary, Edith and Phyllis. Marie Halton, by this time called 'Auntie' by everyone in the family, chose Edith as her protégée. Little Edith would accompany Auntie around Europe, where Marie sang to great acclaim in concert halls and grand houses. Her niece would be required to arrange the items on her dressing table, and woe betide her if she made a mistake or put the pins or powders in the wrong places.

Auntie had many admirers, one of whom was the Duc d'Orléans. She was, indeed, a handsome and subsequently rather terrifying woman.

Occasionally little Edith was sent to school dressed in the white dresses with sashes and big bows in her hair which were the fashion of the time. Mary and Phyllis would join her at school, as long as the money lasted.

Despite this rather interrupted education, all three girls could speak German, French and English. Edith wanted to dance, on the stage. At the age of 16 Auntie sent her to England with a governess to perfect the language, and there it was that my mother persuaded her tutor to allow her to try and become a 'Gaiety Girl'. She succeeded by pretending she was 18, although Auntie soon appeared and put an end to her stage career. However a charming photograph of her in a frilly bonnet is testament to her brief time treading the boards.

My mother was seventeen years old when Auntie decided to take her round England in order to find her a suitable husband. Amongst the families she met were the Edens, who had made their money in County Durham through coal. Years later Daddy told me about the first time my parents had met. "This dreadfully bossy woman appeared, dragging in tow a very young girl wearing the most hideous clothes and a hat which almost entirely concealed her face. When I caught a glimpse of this face, I fell in love immediately and instantly decided to marry her."

My mother's version went like this: "I met Daddy and liked him, but then suddenly I found I was getting married! Daddy decided to change my name to Patricia, as he didn't like Edith."

The Eden family home, Windlestone Hall, was a beautiful house in County Durham. It was presided over by Sybil, Lady Eden. Sybil (née Grey) was a truly beautiful woman who had been painted many times, especially by John Singer Sargent. Her husband, Sir William Eden Bt. had died, and the title of Baronet had therefore been inherited by Timothy, who subsequently became my father.

Sybil, her daughter Marjorie (who was married to the Earl of Warwick) and her younger son Anthony were horrified at my father's decision to marry such a strange little girl from a completely unknown background. No member of my mother's family was invited to the big society wedding, which took place in St. George's Church in Hanover Square, London. The bridesmaids and pages were dressed as mediaeval lords and ladies, and my mother didn't know any of them. I don't think she had a clue about what was happening to her, and she certainly was not allowed to voice any doubts or misgivings. A photograph of her in her shapeless satin pearl-bedecked wedding dress reveals the adorable little face that so enchanted my father.

The first night of my mother's marriage was spent in Warwick Castle, and a grand dinner had been prepared in celebration. My mother had never seen such a large dining table covered with such a bewildering number of glasses and silverware in all her life. Thanks to the kindness of the butler, who whispered instructions to her as to which glass, knife or fork to use, she managed to survive.

My father, Timothy, was one of the most educated, erudite, knowledgeable and well-read of men of his time. I am sure he was filled with loving anticipation at the thought of all the knowledge he was going to impart to his young bride as they toured Europe during the three months of their honeymoon.

A fluent speaker of French and German, Timothy also spoke good Spanish and some Italian. He knew Venice, Rome and Florence as well as any native, as he had studied the art and artists of Europe while living in these cities. He appeared to my mother to know every art gallery and every church or cathedral intimately. He so wanted my mother to share his love, enjoyment and appreciation of all he saw, but sadly, he only succeeded in completely putting her off by trying to do too much at once, and my mother secretly vowed never to visit another art gallery or church again in her life!

After the honeymoon my parents lived at Windlestone Hall. Very soon a daughter, Ann Caroline, was born, but the new mother had no fun with her baby, as she was promptly whisked away by the nurses. The house was run by Sybil, and there was nothing for my mother to do. I expect she passed a great deal of time with her needlework, as she was an excellent seamstress, and loved creating charming clothes for the baby, made out of silks and satins, trimmed with delicate lace and ribbons. To relieve her boredom, she used to whizz up and down the long passages on a scooter that had been given to Ann, somewhat prematurely.

Ann was joined by my brother John. Soon after his birth, while my brother was being breast fed, my father sent word that my mother should hurry up as the funeral for a deceased estate worker was to take place in the private chapel that afternoon. Trying to be as quick as possible after the feeding, my mother grabbed the first hat to hand and dashed into the chapel at the most sombre of moments. All eyes turned towards the breathless young woman who stood panting in the aisle, with a large hat covered in cheerful red cherries bobbing on her head!

By the time Merial Rose was born, my father was coming to the conclusion that it would be no longer viable to retain Windlestone Hall as a family home. To his great sadness, and that of my uncle Anthony, that beautiful house was sold. My parents moved to Hyde Park Gardens in London, and Granny to a small house on the estate.

My mother was not unhappy, as she enjoyed London, and was able to buy a little shop where she was in her element selling frills, ribbons, bows and lace.

Rose was a gorgeous child, with a mass of fair curls and a perfect complexion. She was soon followed by another little girl, Amelia Mary. People stopped my mother in the street to admire this baby, as she had jet-black curls, with the fairest of skin, the bluest of eyes and the dearest little rosebud mouth. A true Snow White indeed.

Another baby was born in 1938. Mary Clare was born a 'blue' baby, and tragically she only lived for three weeks. (As a small child I tried to visualise this phenomenon – in my imagination the poor baby was the brightest blue.) In those days there was no counselling or help with bereavement. My mother was truly devastated and didn't know how to cope, so she left the family home and just disappeared for a while, until she felt able to carry on with her life again.

On going through my mother's possessions after she had died, my sisters and I found a little bundle, tied up in pretty satin ribbon, which contained Mary Clare's baby clothes and the loving and sad letters she had received from my father and Ann and John, who were at a loss as to how to help her. "We still love you – we are still here. Please come home."

Seven years after Amelia had been born, along I came, Elfrida Charlotte, born on the day France fell – 17th June 1940. No blonde or jet black curls, no rosebud mouth – I was destined to disappoint. "My poor little Plainy" my mother was wont to call me in later years, as she bashed a hairbrush 100 times on my head. I accepted the fact that I had beautiful sisters, although it never occurred to me until I was at least seventeen that possibly, just possibly, I could be pretty too.

The years in Canada totally changed my mother, and when she returned to live in England she had developed into a strong and dominant woman. This resulted in some horrendously volatile rows between my parents, although there was no doubt that they loved each other dearly. It was just that they found it hard to live together.

My mother was much too modern for my father. Added to this, was the besetting sin that she was too "American"! I think he forgot that she was indeed half American, but that cut no ice with my father, who blamed all things bad on the influence of the USA.

My mother had phenomenal energy. She would run rather than walk if at all possible. Trailing behind her when she was shopping in Harrods, for example, was a nightmare, and I was always getting lost. She walked her three miniature poodles every day and in between times she would teach at the school she had founded, interview new parents or staff, attend meetings where she often had to look elegant, take me to my dancing classes and then go home and change into old clothes in order to paint school furniture or run up a new pair of curtains if needed, until the small hours of the morning. I think Mummy invented multi-tasking, which was the reason for the question we were always asked – "How does she do it?" In addition to this, when the second school was started at Fritham, she divided her time between the two, which eventually proved too much even for her.

Despite the fact that she and I used to have dreadful rows, which were of course very bruising, we also had the most enormous fun together. I have memories of us laughing and singing ridiculous songs and dancing together anywhere the fancy took us. Mummy could be extremely funny and quite dotty at times,

She was also a very strict mother, who only gave praise when in her opinion it was truly earned. She taught me the need to do my duty before play and to honour my word. She told me about a wonderful actress who was starring in a comedy in the West End even though her little girl was dangerously ill. Sadly the child died during a performance, but the actress finished the play, with everyone laughing at her wit, before rushing to the hospital.

With this doctrine in mind my mother insisted I went to my private ballet class one afternoon, even though I said I was feeling ill. "We can't let your teacher down" she said, and dragged me, feeling perfectly dreadful, up to the bus stop to make the long journey to Cambridge Circus. She believed I was ill about ten minutes into the journey when I was violently sick! We still continued, to tell my teacher, but in a taxi this time. Once home I was lavished with love and care, but she did look a little worried when I was then rushed to hospital with a burst appendix.

My mother was the only person who began to suspect I would grow to a great height. She had heard that gin might slow this progress down, so one day, with Nanny and Mummy looking anxiously on, I was dosed a spoonful of it. I still grew – and I learned to really like gin!

Mummy was not without fault in the way she often dealt with her own children, but of one thing we are all sure, and that is that she loved us utterly and completely and always wanted the very best for us. Sometimes it was hard to be her child, and in many ways she was much better at coping with other people's children, as her standards were not then so high. During her many years she gained much wisdom, which she imparted to us. Even at the end of her life I would ask her advice about how to cope with a difficult situation. The lessons I learned from her stood me in great stead in my eventual career.

Mummy was a woman to be admired. Coming from her unusual background she achieved so much. The Americans adored her, and to this day I still meet girls who had been at her schools and who remember her with great affection, and not a little fear occasionally. If I conjure up her image now, I see a smiling, loving, interested, amusing, wonderful woman.

★ ★ ★

It is hard to remember when I first saw my father. I was nearly four years old when we returned from Canada, and we were bombed out quite soon after. We then lived in the New Forest and my father was still working in the War Office in London.

I was dimly conscious of this tall, rather severe man making brief appearances in my life, but it wasn't until I was well into my seventh year that I began to get to know this extraordinary, unusual, extremely talented man.

Timothy Calvert was born on 13th May 1893 to Sir William and Lady Eden from County Durham. Tim was their second son, the eldest being John, or Jack as he was known. Jack was a brave and gallant soldier who lost his life in France at the beginning of WW1. He lies buried in the Royal British Legion war cemetery near Ypres.

My father also lost his youngest brother Nicholas, during this war. At the age of only 16 he died during the Battle of Jutland on board the *Indefatigable,* on which he was serving as a midshipman. William and Sybil, my grandparents, were devastated at their loss, as were my father, his brother Anthony and their elder sister Elfrida Marjorie.

Grandfather William was an eccentric who was also an extremely talented water colourist and amateur boxer. His fierce temper was legendary. My father in later years wrote a charming biography of William entitled *The Tribulations Of A Baronet,* in which he recounted many anecdotes relating to his temper, including a famous quarrel he had with the well-known painter Rex Whistler.

Upon the death of Sir William my father inherited the Baronetcy, the family home Windlestone Hall and horrific death duties. After valiantly trying to keep the estate viable, he made the sad decision to sell the beautiful house the family loved so much.

The only memory I have of Windlestone is visiting Park House, where my grandmother lived until her death in 1945, and finding yellow raspberries in the garden, which my sister and I then proceeded to throw up to the kitchen ceiling, to see who could make the largest 'splat'!

Daddy was extremely strict about our good behaviour, manners and timekeeping. When he entered a room where we might be playing, we would instantly have to stand up and greet him politely.

When we lived in Fritham House we had a family of Italians working for us in the house and garden. Two of the men were trained to be butlers, with a modicum of success. We had a large brass gong, and Salvatore would beat this gong fifteen minutes before a meal and then again when the meal was ready. No excuse would be accepted for a late or untidy arrival.

It was unusual to say the least, but my father lived in his charming little flat over the stable yard, while my mother had her bedroom in the main house. In the way of children, I totally accepted this strange state of affairs. My sisters Rose and Amelia and I all had rooms in the attic, which we adored. Sometimes we would look out of the library window to see Daddy coming across the garden for lunch. He would be swathed in his voluminous blue cloak, and as he strode along the path, we would try to gauge what sort of mood he would be in. If bad, we would all be on terribly good behaviour. If good, we often would have the most enormous fun at table, playing word games.

Meal times were either a pleasure or a trial. We would sit at the large dining room table, which could seat 16, with the family silver on display. Children were "seen and not heard". We were not allowed to fidget, and fingers were placed on the table when we were not eating. My mother had the charming habit of creeping up behind us with a fork, which she would prod into our backs if we were not sitting up straight. Oh what cruelty – but somehow we survived without turning into demonic child abusers ourselves.

My father was a conundrum. He was such a complex

character in every way. Stickler as he was for punctuality and good behaviour, he also had a wonderful sense of mischief. When Amelia and I were about 14 and 21, with Papa's full approval, we played a practical joke on my godfather, who was lunching with us together with his parents, son and son's friend. My godfather was Sir Dudley Forwood and he had been Equerry to the Duke of Windsor at the time of his abdication. He told us many a fascinating story about this period, although he was always discreet.

Daddy had recently produced a play with the pupils at the school called *The Nun's Story*. Amelia and I dressed up in two of the white habits, and my parents referred to us as Sister Agnes and Sister Teresa. My mother asked us to say the grace before the meal, and we were so amused that my somewhat naughty and irreverent godfather totally refused to talk to us. The young male guest, in contrast, plied me with questions and asked me which order I was from. "Little Sisters of the Poor", I immediately replied. After lunch Mia and I went to our rooms and changed back into jeans. We danced into the library, where we were greeted with roars of laughter by all except the young man. Poor fellow, he had been completely taken in, and as a devout Roman Catholic he took a dim view of our antics.

Years later I met him again when I was pregnant with my first child. "I know you are not really having a baby," he said, "I am sure that is a balloon!"

My father had been studying in Germany when WW1 had broken out and he was immediately interned in a prisoner-of-war camp in Ruhleben. He always felt guilty that he had been captured so early and was safe, while all his brothers were fighting. My Uncle Anthony has described his experiences in the trenches with great vividness in his autobiography *Another*

World. During his time in the camp Papa did some acting, and found he had a talent. After the war he joined the famous actress Mrs Patrick Campbell and her troupe, as well as appearing in Godfrey Tearle's production of *Hamlet* in the West End.

In subsequent years his talent for drama emerged as a playwright and producer. His play *Saul Of Tarsus* which was performed by the pupils of Fritham House School, was a triumph, and he coaxed performances out of young girls that resulted in grown men shedding tears.

Thanks to his acting talent, Daddy was a brilliant storyteller. Mystery and ghost stories were the best. It was a total pleasure to listen to him reading aloud, and he introduced us to books from a bygone age that thrilled or enchanted us. The author H Rider Haggard was a firm favourite. *Montezuma's Daughter* and *King Solomon's Mines* were so exciting. The Victorian author Mrs Molesworth had us weeping copiously at the sad tales of poor little children dying needlessly but oh so bravely.

When I was very young our favourite were the Golliwog books. Not politically correct nowadays, but how we loved the adventures of these dolls. Goll was immensely brave, and he and fearless Sarah Jane, along with Meg and Peg the twins and tiny little Midget, had the most brilliant adventures. We would curl up on the enormous purple velvet sofa (six of us could fit easily) in the library to hear the next instalment. Daddy would be seated in his favourite chair before a roaring fire, and the light from the flames would catch the gold print and bindings on the magnificent collection of leather-bound books arranged on the floor-to-ceiling shelves in the library.

The library was indeed my father's domain. Here he would write sitting at the elegant writing table in the centre of the room. Silver inkwells contained different-coloured inks, and the rocking blotter was much in use. Opposite the sofa was an Elizabethan refectory table made out of a single oak tree and at least twelve feet long.

It was also in this room that my father introduced us to classical music. He had a brilliant collection of records, but the only problem was we were not allowed to talk. Being as naughty as I was, I would write notes and pull faces without allowing myself to listen. I eventually discovered the beauty of music by myself years later.

My mother used to say that my father had too many talents, and did not excel in any of them. He was indeed a gifted amateur painter. His portraits were often excellent and his trees were beautiful. Sadly in later life his disappointments reflected themselves in his paintings, which duly became darker and more sombre as the years passed.

Undoubtedly his greatest talent was writing. He published a charming book called *Five Dogs And Two More*, and his biography of his father was received to great acclaim. He also completed two volumes on County Durham for the County Book series.

The worst thing for us children was when Daddy liked something we were wearing. "That's a pretty blouse" he might say, "Come to my studio at two this afternoon. I want to paint you in it." One day when I was six years old he said that to me when I was wearing a small Swiss cap. I had particular plans for that afternoon; a serious amount of tree climbing and then a good game of hide and seek. It was a beautiful day, and the last thing I wanted to do was sit still while Daddy drew me.

To cheer me up, Papa insisted that Amelia came and read to me at the same time. My dear sister had a raging temper when roused, and she was furious. She read to me in the crossest and nastiest of voices, and I listened with the sulkiest of faces. The ensuing charming sketch in charcoal captures this misery so well, and it hangs in my house as a permanent reminder of that day.

When I was six and living in London, Daddy arrived from the country to celebrate his and Mummy's wedding anniversary. For this occasion I had learned *Daffodils* by Wordsworth to recite to my father as a surprise. I was dressed in my best party dress, and clutching a bunch of daffodils.

As the front door opened, before Daddy could even get inside, I began "I wandered lonely as a…" before Mummy interrupted and told me to wait a bit. So I waited while he took his coat off, and I began again. Twice more I attempted to say my poem, until finally, laughing, my parents managed to sit down and listen to me.

He was, at this time, virtually unknown to me, and I remember looking at him curiously.

I was often asked to perform little poems and songs for the grown-ups, and one I recall with a feeling of total revulsion, was called *Good Night*. It was sickly in the extreme and I performed it while holding a doll. *"Nurse put the light out – for I must rest. Good night Mama, Good night Papa, but* (with a big hug) *I still love my dolly best. Good night –* (fainter) *good night."* And there I would lie with my eyes tight shut, listening to the friends of my parents murmuring how sweet I was!

After that I really associated Daddy with life at Fritham. On one occasion when my Uncle Anthony was visiting, I saw the two men walking along the path by the orchard. They were very alike, and both were tall and handsome. For an awful moment I couldn't tell which one was which. I stood still and stared at them (I must have been five years old), and my father, jokingly, pulled a mad face and roared. I was totally terrified and turned tail and ran! Uncle Anthony thought this was so hilarious that he gave me a £1 note later as compensation. This started the trend, and he kindly gave me £1 every time I saw him, even when I visited him in hospital. I had no conception at that time how famous my uncle was (he was the Foreign Secretary then). He was just Uncle Anthony to me and I really enjoyed chatting to him. It was also very sad for him that his eldest son, Simon, had died at the very end of the war in Burma. Years later on a visit to this country, my brother John found Simon's grave.

There is no doubt that Uncle Anthony was a very charming and intelligent man. In subsequent years I learned that many attractive women had fallen for these charms, and it was just as well that in 1952 he married Clarissa Churchill, who managed to keep him in control!

Christmas time was very special. A huge tree from the forest dominated the drawing room and was lit by real candles. A bucket of water was nearby in case of fire. Daddy would play the piano and we would sing carols around the tree before going to bed on Christmas Eve with our stockings.

On Christmas Day after church and a huge lunch we would play parlour games. Charades was the great favourite, and *Here We Go Gathering Nuts In May*. I don't think Christmas has ever been so exciting since.

We went to church every Sunday when we were in the New Forest, and we always had to wear a hat and gloves. The services were often long and boring, so we would play the alphabet game during the sermons, which helped pass the time!

I used to be very sad when I looked at the tiny grave where my baby sister, Mary Clare, lay buried. Her headstone was engraved with this charming poem by Robert Herrick:

HERE A PRETTY BABY LIES
SUNG ASLEEP WITH LULLABIES
PRAY BE SILENT, DO NOT STIR
THE EASY EARTH THAT COVERS HER.

I used to dream about Mary Clare. She was my own special angel, and she would have been the most wonderful friend to me. She would not have been mean to me, as my brother and other sisters often were. I would gaze at her little grave and long for her to be alive. Years later, my sister Rose wrote a most beautiful poem in her memory for our parents. Part of it goes as follows:-

> *Perhaps because you were too frail for sorrow*
> *No love could tempt you here on earth to stay.*
> *Nor mortal toys, nor mortal tears persuade you.*
> *We loved the more knowing you would not stay.*
> *'Tis strange that one should be so long remembered*
> *The purpose of whose life we could not guess.*
> *Yet in that brief time enviously we gathered*
> *Memories enough to cheat forgetfulness.*

Mary Clare's death had a profound effect on both my parents. Sadly I realised I was not destined to be the little angel she undoubtedly would have been.

My father was a man out of his time. His generation went from the horse-drawn carriage to the first man on the moon, and it was too much to take in. He yearned for the genteel orderly life of his youth, the slower pace of life, the art of letter writing, time for intelligent conversation, and above all – NO television! He abhorred every modern invention, except perhaps the telephone. His letters were a joy to receive.

My proudest moment was when he made the effort to see me perform in a production of *The Boy Friend* at the Hornchurch Theatre in Essex. He adored the show, and was proud of me. I also did some choreography for one of his plays at Fritham, and he was surprised and delighted at how well I was able to do this.

In subsequent years, when I had particularly aggravated my mother, she would say in exasperation, "Oh you are so like your father!" He was a wonderful man, if a difficult one. A tremendously loving man who adored all children, especially his own.

There were many times when we grumbled at his strictness and his anger was positively terrifying, as he did not 'spare the rod' unfortunately. On one occasion when I was about six years old I had displeased him and knew I was about to be severely punished. I decided to run away from him through the house. Daddy chased after me, and I darted about as quickly as I could between the front and back stairs running down the long corridors. On descending the front stairs I suddenly saw him standing at the bottom. He was fuming with fury. I stopped in my tracks, put my hands on my hips, and said in my crossest of voices, "Don't you stand there staring at me like that, you nasty, bad-tempered old man!"

My father's reaction summed him up. He totally collapsed with laughter, and I rushed into his arms, where we both gave each other a huge hug.

He was a wonderful man who was often troubled, but he taught us all so much and has left us a legacy of letters, paintings and books to keep his memory alive.

★ ★ ★

My brother and my two eldest sisters were somewhat distant figures in my early childhood. Being seventeen years older than I, Ann, always referred to by me as my Great Big Sister Ann, was immensely grown up and a bit scary. It would be many a year before we established the lovely friendship that I now treasure.

I was thrilled to be her bridesmaid, and even more excited at the age of twelve to become an aunt. Being brought up never to put elbows on dining tables unless one was over 21 or an aunt afforded me great joy, as I now ostentatiously plonked my elbows on tables, assuring everyone it was quite all right, as I was an aunt!

Ann married Peter Negretti, whose family owned a famous camera and binocular shop in Bond St called Negretti and Zambra. It was Peter who gave me my first proper camera. This was extremely kind of him, considering I had nearly killed my beloved little niece a short time before. I was staying with Ann and Peter, and helping with the baby. Ann allowed me to take her for a walk in her smart Silver Cross baby carriage. Unfortunately I headed towards a steep hill, and the pram became too heavy for me. I jogged to try and catch it up – but it went faster. I ran as fast as I could, but knew I couldn't hold it, so I steered towards a grassy bank, and the pram, with little Alexandra inside it, tipped right over.

Luckily a car stopped at once. The passengers helped me, and to our relief the baby was unhurt. The pram was a bit scratched though, and I was terrified at the thought of telling my Great Big Sister. Fortunately she was so relieved that the baby had survived that she didn't mind about the pram at all.

My sister had four wonderful daughters, although tragically her darling Emma died of cancer aged 21. Ann's strong character helped her through this dreadful period and indeed has stood her in good stead all her life. She is now known in our family as 'Saint Ann', as she is always ready to help in times of need.

John was another shadowy childhood figure. He dipped in and out, sometimes in army fatigues accompanied by his faithful Basenji dog. It wasn't until he decided to try to become an MP that I began to get to know him properly. I helped him canvass for support in Paddington, where although he didn't win, he reduced the Labour majority so much that he received a telegram of congratulations from Sir Winston Churchill.

John ultimately became the youngest MP in the House. He represented Bournemouth West, and during his parliamentary career became Minister of State for Industry in 1970 and Minister for Post and Telecommunications in 1972. He was elevated to the House of Lords in 1983.

Whenever John was in the house there was always laughter. I thought he was totally wonderful, and though he pretty much ignored me as a child, I hero-worshipped him and thought that he and our cousin Jimmy Stockley were the best-looking boys in the world.

John firstly married Belinda Pascoe and they had four children, Emily, Charlotte, Robert and Jack. The marriage was dissolved and he met his second wife, Margaret Ann, when she came to view the lovely house in Wiltshire he was sadly selling. They ended up living together in the house for many happy years.

With the help of Margaret Ann, herself a wonderfully talented painter, they ran Lady Eden's School until it was bought by Thomas's London Day Schools.

My brother's charming nickname for me as a child was "Awful Eiffel", as I was almost as tall as the Eiffel Tower! I had no nickname for him. I just adored him.

Rose was another sibling who dipped in and out of my life, although thanks to her brilliance on the piano I was much more aware of her. Lying in my room above the drawing room at night, I would listen to her playing, and thought I would never hear anything more beautiful. Later on she often played for my ballet lessons.

Everything Rose did she did well. She was different from the rest of us. With blond curly hair and sharper features, Rose looked like an Eden from a bygone period. Rose had a fantastic brain, and she and my father would have the most terrifying competitions at meal times, flinging quotes at each other to see who would falter first.

I adored my sister Rose, for when she did appear, she would tell me the most wonderful made-up stories, always about incredibly naughty children or animals that got the better of humans. She could draw and paint and make beautiful doll's clothes. Rose and Amelia would ride their half-Arab horses in the New Forest, sometimes dressed in Bedouin clothes. On one special occasion she took me on my bumbling pony deep into the forest for a picnic, which was a never-to-be-forgotten experience.

Rose married Dalton Murray, a diplomat, and after he died she took herself off to a remote part of southern France, with glorious views of the Pyrenees, where for a while she made use of her other talent, photography. If she had desired it Rose could have made a fortune with her photography, showing once again a fantastic gift for beauty, humour, charm and pathos. She chose not to, but luckily the photos live on.

My sadness was that I did not see enough of Rose, and as our lives progressed, we saw even less of each other. Rose had a wicked sense of humour, and was universally loved by all our children and grandchildren. It is such a tragedy that this immensely talented and extraordinary woman should have succumbed to dementia in the last part of her life.

Amelia, my closest sister in age and my greatest friend, needs a book to herself! My sister made headlines when she married Giovanni Borrelli in 1958. It was hard to decide who got the most publicity then, Elizabeth Taylor and Richard Burton, who were marrying on Capri, or Amelia Eden, who was married on the next-door island of Ischia!

Sadly the marriage didn't last, but they had three wonderful children and seven grandchildren. Amelia's heart and home have always been in the New Forest. As children, she and Rose kept many ponies as well as their beautiful horses Ishak and Rudan. Together they would go to the Beaulieu sales, where young horses were being sold for meat, and buy as many as they could for £5 each. I would then be roped in to help them while these ponies were broken, groomed and fed properly so that eventually they could go to a good home as children's ponies.

Amelia was utterly fearless, and I admired her a great deal, despite the fact that she could be horrible to me. I was easy to trick, being so much younger, but I should have suspected something when she sweetly gave me a huge spoonful of whipped cream, only for me to discover it was shampoo!

After the war we had a surplus of blackout curtains. Amelia told me one day a gypsy was coming to tell our fortunes. I was to present myself at the door of our playroom at 10 o'clock and not before.

On entering the pitch-black room, I dimly made out a tent, and from inside I heard the querulous voice of an old woman inviting me in. Nervously I took a seat. I could just see colourful scarves and jangly decorations; this was definitely an old gypsy woman. She then proceeded to give me ghastly news. I would be sick, I would never be a dancer, I would never marry – in fact nothing nice at all. I rushed out of the room in floods of tears, straight into the arms of Nanny.

"Gypsy woman my eye!" said Nanny as she burst into the room. She brought out from the 'tent' my sister, most beautifully dressed as a gypsy, but grimacing in pain from the fierce hand of Nanny as she was dragged off to see our mother. Despite her punishment, I think Mia thought it was all worthwhile.

Amelia and I climbed trees together and explored the forest, the grounds, the airfield and the attics. We loved each other really. A good game was "Nobody must see us". We had to get from one end of the village to the other without anyone seeing us. We thought it was huge fun. We adored rolling down hills, and used to race each other to the bottom. We also collected snails, and I had forgotten one day that I had some in my pocket as we careered down the hill. The subsequent squidgy mess put me off rolling for a while.

I think my grandchildren would think we were quite mad, as they sit with their electronic games and modern sophistications. Our pleasures were quite inexpensive.

CHAPTER FOUR

HOLIDAYS AT HOME
AND ABROAD

Holidays abroad did not feature largely in my childhood, which undoubtedly was a blessing – if disguised. A normal holiday for me was leaving London for the New Forest. I was always excited as I anticipated the journey and my subsequent joy at being back in Fritham. We travelled by train – in style. My mother would book her habitual Pullman carriage B. The white-coated steward would be waiting by the door to greet us and help my mother, me and the three poodles to our places. We would either have a light luncheon or afternoon tea with hot buttered tea cakes, all served on the white-clothed table on china plates.

At Southampton our 'own' taxi would be waiting for us, and I would crane my neck in anticipation trying to get the first glimpse of the house as we rounded the last bend.

Once at Fritham, as soon as I was able, I raced out into the gardens and ran as fast as I could in any and every direction. I would then say "hello" to all my favourite trees – especially the cedar tree, which I would immediately climb, and then hang upside on a branch for as long as I could. I was in heaven!

I grew to learn to love the forest and Amelia and I would walk the dogs for hours. When I was a little older I would escape into the deepest part I could find, with a rug and something delicious to read, and hide there for hours. I was never missed.

My last night at Fritham would invariably see me in tears – but then gradually the excitement of returning to London began to envelop me.

Once back in London, I would absorb the sounds of the city. The distant hooting of the boats on the Thames; the clatter of hooves made by the milkman's pony; people walking past the house chatting, and even the sounds of cars, which in those days did not drown the songs of the birds. I was happy in London as well.

Our first overseas holiday in 1946 was amazingly with our mother alone, as my father elected to stay at home.

Mummy and I, together with my elder sisters, Rose and Amelia, went to the small mountain village of Glion, above Montreux in Switzerland. We stayed in a large house which was the home of the prince and princess of somewhere in Europe. I remember them as being kind, elderly, and not the least bit like a prince or princess.

We were met off the train by the prince himself driving an ancient (even then) 'sit up and beg' car. This poor little car panted and strained as it slowly groaned its way up the mountainous road. Finally we ground to a halt, just by a cascading little brook tumbling down the side of the mountain. The driver got out of the car with a watering can in his hand and filled this with water, which he duly poured into the car under the open bonnet. My mother and I watched with fascination, but she was far more impressed than I. "How amazing" she said, "a car that runs on water! Why don't we have those in England?"

Our house (or palace, as I called it to myself) was large with unbelievable views. It had a wide veranda, and we sat on this for our breakfast the next day.

The house had a small farm attached to it, and the young farmer. whom we knew as Bobby, was devastatingly good looking. I totally fell in love with him, but unfortunately so did my beautiful sister Rose, and as I was only six years old, I rather lost out. However, Bobby let me ride his enormous grey farm horse, and I was also allowed to play with the several rabbits which were kept in cages by the stables. I had a favourite, whom I called Smokey, and every morning I would rush to release him and play with him in the grass.

One day Smokey's cage was empty. I found Bobby.

"Where is my rabbit?" I demanded.

"Oh, we had him for supper last night," was the reply. "He was excellent."

My love for Bobby diminished instantly, and I cried copiously for my furry friend.

My dear sister Amelia nearly killed me on this holiday. As she was thirteen at the time and I was only six, she ought to have known better, as she later admitted. However, at that time, Amelia was the most daring and daredevil of sisters and I was always being the wimp, although I did try to keep up with her.

Day after sunny day she and I would sit on the rolling bank of the grassy meadow, reading, talking and drawing pictures in the sun on each other's backs. Below us there was a small railway line, and every so often we would watch in fascination as a little mountain train wound its way along the rails before disappearing into a deep tunnel.

"Let's go and see the tunnel" suggested Amelia. Of course I agreed. I didn't want to appear a 'scaredy cat' so down we went, and holding hands, ventured into the dark abyss.

I was afraid – I admit it. I expect Amelia was as well. In fact, when we felt the rails beginning to tremble and 'sing' we were both terrified, as we knew that meant a train would arrive very soon.

"Quick!" said Mia, "we must get out before the train gets here." We stumbled along in the dark, keeping our eyes fixed on the light at the end. The noise became louder, and we very nearly made it – but not quite. The train came charging along, and Amelia and I pressed back against the wall of the tunnel. As the train thundered past, we could see the faces of the passengers lit up. One man saw us too. He shook his fist at us. As soon as the train had passed we scampered back to the house as quickly as we could. Both of us were severely shaken by this experience.

After this we confined our activities to picking flowers and being good. At least we were good for the last few days in Glion. This was the only holiday abroad I remember when my mother was present from start to finish. We loved it.

A happy memory I have of a holiday when my father was present was during our first visit to Frinton-on-Sea, when I was eight years old. We were on the beach, well wrapped up against the cold wind, and my father was helping me to build a really splendid sandcastle. Images come to mind of a somewhat chilly summer, when I am sure my mottled blue skin resembled the equally mottled blue of my bubbly swimsuit. We had a beachside hut, and I would rush there, dripping with salty water after pretending to swim in the sea, in order to be vigorously rubbed down with a towel by Nanny before being given a welcome cup of cocoa from a thermos flask.

When the following year my mother told me we were to return to Frinton, I was filled with excitement. Several of our friends were to meet us there and best of all, I was booked on a course of private tennis lessons.

Our first week was memorable for two reasons. The first was I learned how to swim, and the second was the Fancy Dress Parade.

My mother had tried with my swimming, and to give her her due she really thought it was important that I should learn. To this end I had a series of lessons in the amazing Art Deco swimming pool in the bowels of the earth, underneath the prestigious Grosvenor House Hotel in Park Lane, London.

As I approached the pool down a series of sloping passages, the sounds of happy shouting children and the strong smell of chlorine invaded my senses. I was filled with nervous anticipation. My instructor was a rather severe man who wore a white shirt and long white trousers rolled up at the ankles. The only concession he made to being near water was the fact that he wore no socks or shoes, otherwise he didn't deign to let himself get wet. I would be in the water holding one end of a rope while he held the other and pulled me from one side of the pool, all the while shouting instructions. I had no idea what he was talking about and valiantly tried to imitate his arm and leg movements, to no avail. After my lessons I would adopt a strange crouching position as I walked in the water trying to pretend I was swimming and utterly convinced I was fooling everybody as I flailed my arms about. This was why, for the second year running, I arrived at Frinton-on-Sea unable to swim.

I was playing in the sea with my friend Sally when she noticed I was not swimming. She was incredulous at my inability and told me she could teach me at once. This she duly did, in about five minutes, by teaching me how to float.

Together with the majority of our friends we were made temporary members of the tennis club, and during our first week this club held a party and fancy dress competition.

The previous term at our school, Lady Eden's School, we had staged a rather magnificent production of *La Boutique Fantasque*. One of the costumes used was that of a French poodle, and my mother had brought this outfit for me to wear at the party. It was an excellent costume in white, with 'poodle' wool round my thighs, wrists and ankles and a brilliant headdress with long ears and a poodle pom-pom. I truly felt I had a good chance of winning a prize.

After the fun of the party, the judging was announced. Girls came first in reverse order. No 3 – 'Little Bo Peep, No 2 – A Fairy Ballerina, and the winner was a boring mediaeval princess. I couldn't believe it. I was miserable, but I still had to stand there while they announced the results for the boys. No 3 – Oliver Twist, No 2 – Peter Pan and the winner is – the French poodle!

I was propelled forward to receive the first prize for boys and as I collected it, I stammered that I was in fact, a girl. Little did I know that due to my height and somewhat skinny frame this would not be the only time I would be mistaken for a boy.

Far better than winning the fancy dress competition, however, was the fact that I was learning to play tennis. I absolutely loved the lessons I had every morning, and passionately adored my instructor. Despite panicking that I would develop telltale muscles in my right arm which would affect my ballet career, I have loved and enjoyed the game of tennis all my life, and still in my dotage play whenever I can.

My father joined us during the second week, bringing with him a little girl called Caroline and her mother, Daphne. Caroline's mother was a war widow and had been recently engaged by my parents to be a housemistress at Fritham House School. I liked Caroline. She was a year older than I was and I felt so sorry for her not having a father. I have to admit that I did not initially feel the same about her mother, as she rather frightened me. I suspect I was aware that like the other two widowed mothers with girls my age who worked in our school, she was a bit jealous of me. These ladies undoubtedly resented all the good things I had which due to their unfortunate circumstances were denied their own daughters. This was not my fault, of course, but between them in subsequent years they all made sure I knew how they felt.

My father, obviously with the best of intentions, tried to rectify this situation, but in a rather harsh way. The day after they had arrived I turned up for my tennis lesson as usual to find Caroline already on the court, being watched by her mother. I asked when her lessons would be finished, only to be told by an embarrassed tennis coach that I was to have no more lessons, as Caroline was taking my place.

I was mortified and terribly disappointed, although the biggest hurt was the knowledge that my father had arranged for Caroline to have my lessons with no word to me or my mother. The thought that we might have shared the lessons apparently did not occur to him. I retired hurt and miserable and my mother did her best to comfort me, although she must have been feeling equally angry herself.

★ ★ ★

Daphne and Caroline became part of our extended family for a while, so it was no surprise that they came on holidays with us. Somehow Daphne always chose the venue. The first time we went to Val André in Brittany, which was good fun. The following year we headed off to the Hotel du Lac in Hossegore, close to Biarritz in the South of France, and to my joy my mother said she would come as well as my sisters, Rose and Amelia.

Journeys to Europe with my father were always enjoyable, as we did everything in such style. Everywhere we went we were met by a Thomas Cook representative. Naturally we travelled first class on the Golden Arrow in England and La Flèche d'Or in France. For the journey to Biarritz we had the super adventure of travelling in an overnight sleeper train. It was impossible to sleep with all the clangs and rattles, but even so our excitement wasn't dimmed when we peeped out of the windows early next morning to view the mountains etched against the lightening sky. However, by the time we had taken three trains and a boat and the final taxi had deposited us at the Hotel du Lac, we were all hot, bothered and exhausted.

Daphne had filled our imagination with descriptions of a beautiful hotel on the shores of a large lake, and we couldn't wait to see it. Our rooms were not ready for us, so we were ushered into a decidedly charmless and bleak dining room. We looked out of the windows to view the lake, but all we could see were miles of muddy-looking sand and a strip of water way in the distance. The lake turned out to be tidal, and when the tide was out, it wasn't there. There was however a strip of dry sand, and Caroline and I were allowed to take off our socks and shoes and go onto this beach. We decided to walk out onto the mud, where trickles of water were beginning to return to the shore. I had not gone far when my foot struck something extremely painful. I let out a sharp cry as I saw I had stepped on a large jagged piece of glass.

My foot was pouring blood as I hobbled up the steps to the dining room for help. I was immediately castigated for trailing blood all over the floor, and this set the tone for what turned out to be the most miserable holiday of my life.

My mother managed to get me into the village, where we found a doctor. I am sure I should have had stitches, but he assured me that with a good firm bandage my foot should heal in no time, provided I kept it dry. I could hardly believe it, as keeping it dry meant no playing in the water. To cheer me up Mummy bought me a red inflatable boat. She thought I could bob around in that while at the same time keeping my foot dry.

The hotel was hideous, and we all hated it. After two days Mummy announced that she was returning to England. It might have been kind, in view of my wounded foot, if she had taken me as well, but she left me behind to be looked after by Daddy and Daphne. Rose and Amelia did their own things and stayed out of our way. Before she left Mummy told me I was to travel in my white skirt, blue blazer and boater for the return journey. So strange to think of this nowadays when the only criteria for travelling clothes seems to be comfort or scruff order, but in those days people did dress up to travel.

I cried buckets when Mummy left, and then sat disconsolately on the beach while I had to endure watching

Caroline larking about in my little red boat. Daphne took over the care of my foot, but refused to do a tight bandage and complained to my father I was ungrateful, as I wanted her to do it like the doctor had told us. I was severely reprimanded and made to go to my room, even though it was a glorious day.

I would cry myself to sleep every night, but would always wake up in the small hours. Daddy and I shared a room on the ground floor which opened onto a tiny garden. Silently I would creep out of the room and find a deckchair to sit on. Soon I would be joined by a decidedly scruffy but loving dog. He would clamber up onto my lap, and he and I would give each other much-needed love and cuddles until the first hint of dawn gradually appeared.

One day we had an excursion to Bayonne. We were excited, as there was a fair there and we were greatly looking forward to it. We reckoned without my father though, who insisted Caroline and I should have an afternoon rest and booked us a hotel room in order that we should spend a quiet afternoon. We were both utterly fed up, and spent the next couple of hours having jumping competitions on the bed.

Finally we were allowed up, and given ice creams in a café. Daddy told us he had been shopping for us, and he presented Caroline with a wonderful camera. I was thrilled, as I felt sure I would have one too. To own a camera was immensely grown up. Alas I did not get a camera, but a little china ornament of flowers. I tried hard to hide my disappointment.

Every day I asked Daphne if I could swim, and every day the answer was no. I was incredibly bored and just sat on the small strip of sand jealously watching Caroline in the water. Towards the end of the holiday I was in my usual place when a friendly young couple came to talk to me. They said they had felt sorry for me seeing I was having no fun on my own, and they suggested they should take me for a ride in their rowing boat. I was worried about getting my foot wet, but the man said he would carry me, and then they would wrap my foot in a towel so it would keep quite dry.

It was glorious sitting on that boat and getting out on the water for the first time in ten days. I was chatting away to this sweet couple when to my horror I saw my father at the window of our room, gesticulating in wild fury that I should return at once.

After I had been carried safely back to the beach I braved my father, who berated me for my dreadful disobedience and unbelievable rudeness to Daphne, who had been taking such care of my foot. "But I didn't get it wet" I wailed, "Let me see" said my father. He felt my foot and pronounced it wet, and sent me behind the curtain to our primitive washing area to dry it at once. I waved the towel around but didn't touch my foot. "That's better" pronounced my father, and then promptly sent me to Daphne to apologise for my disobedience. I also had to promise not to speak to the nice young couple again.

The last straw was when Daphne refused to allow me to wear the clothes Mummy had chosen for me on the journey home, as she wanted me to look like Caroline. It is true to say I fairly hated her then!

How strange it is that years later I was a bridesmaid at Caroline's wedding, and actually became very fond of Daphne and enjoyed visiting her in her latter years. I bear no grudge, but the scars of that miserable and thankfully last family holiday remain.

Curiously my love for my father was never affected, and during his lifetime I did my best to please him and make him proud of me. I never blamed Caroline either. The situation was no fault of hers, and we are friends to this day.

CHAPTER FIVE

LADY EDEN'S SCHOOL

In 1946 my mother, Patricia, Lady Eden, decided that because she could find no school that was suitable for me, she would simply start her own.

"They were all so dreary" she told me later, "cream and green or brown and beige. I wanted a *pretty* school and then the children would *want* to learn."

My mother found a suitable house in Kensington. It was empty at the time, but fortunately a basement window was conveniently left unlocked. Carefully removing her precious nylon stockings, she prised the window open and squeezed herself through it. She then toured the house, which she instantly knew was perfect.

The house, in Victoria Road, was highly unusual in that it had a magnificent central double height hall, with a small staircase leading up to a gallery and studio room. Originally this had been a huge barn, and the pulleys for hauling up bales of hay to the attic store rooms were still in place.

My father was persuaded, and the house was duly bought. Initially we lived in it as a family, and used a second large room which connected with the old barn as our drawing room. The idea for a school was discussed and approved. My eldest sister Ann was instrumental in setting up the business side of the project. My mother advertised for teachers, and promptly turned down anyone who turned up in a 'worthy hat' or 'sensible' shoes. Somehow like-minded, inspirational and non-conventional teachers appeared, and the school started life in 1947 with seven pupils, of which I was one.

The central hall/barn-cum-ballroom was the hub of school life. Lessons were taken sitting at little round tables. These were then covered with tablecloths for lunch, after which they were folded away for games, drill and most importantly, ballet lessons. In no time at all pupil numbers doubled, trebled and quadrupled. Other rooms in the house were commandeered to become classrooms. Mummy would work late into the evenings painting diminutive wooden tables and chairs in cheery colours. She made curtains in fun fabrics for the windows and the walls were hung with bright and colourful pictures. The little girls wore French-style gingham pinafores, and gradually a uniform emerged, in blue, white and grey. A young friend had just bought a knitting machine, so she was given the job of knitting navy blue leggings and matching 'sausage' hats with bobbles. (Little did she know what a trendsetter she was, as in years to come several schools copied the 'sausage' hats with bobbles!)

My mother taught us Geography. We would chant – "Turkey – Syria – Trans Jordan. Iraq – Iran – Afghanistan" while learning about the Middle East. They were just names of countries to us children. No impending doom was associated with them then. They all seemed magical and mysterious. Now, oh what horrors and sadness are conjured up by that little chant.

The huge shiny atlas, with all the pink bits showing the countries that 'belonged' to us (the smallest of them all) was taken off the wall and formed into an inward-facing circle which we, standing in the middle, slowly spun round to give us an understanding of the world being round.

My mother also taught French, and eventually she wrote her own French grammar textbook. As she had learned German, French and English at an early age, the French language was taught from the first form upwards by native French speakers. Games were played and songs were sung, while only French was spoken at the French table at lunchtime. Soon the school's reputation for teaching French spread far and wide. Lady Eden's girls always took the 12+ or 13+ exams when they were only 11.

My early days at LES were enriched by the most inspirational teacher of all time. She started with us as Miss Hayes and later became Lady Bethune. Miss Hayes opened our eyes not only to English History, Literature and Language but to the wonders of Greek Mythology and Architecture, Astrology, History of Art and Poetry.

We acted out every scenario we possibly could, whether it was a tragic Greek tale or a poem such as *How They Brought the Good News from Ghent to Aix*. We could not wait for her lessons to learn more. Spelling tests; composition writing; Bible stories or history were all brought alive for us, and we were truly lucky children to find learning and discovery such an exciting adventure.

Miss Hayes was loved by us all. I could not bear to displease her, but once she had to comfort me as I had done something wrong, and I was inconsolable with grief. Alerted by my mother, who could nothing with me, Miss Hayes found me in my bedroom, dressed only in my vest and pants. She sat me on her knee and assured me she still loved me, and what I had done (lost in the mists of time) was not so serious. For many years to come, long after Miss Hayes had become Lady Bethune and was Mary to me, we would recollect that little scene, and try to envisage the fact that at five foot ten I had EVER been small enough to sit upon her petite knee!

Mary Hayes formed a wonderful partnership with Peggy Ayers, who was our ballet teacher. Peggy had come to us from the famous Vera Volkova studio. Together they created some wonderful shows, with undoubtedly the best being *The Rape Of The Lock* by Alexander Pope, adapted by Mary. Peggy choreographed some stunning dance sequences, and the outstanding costumes were all made by an enormously talented seamstress called Clarice Chater. The costumes were works of art themselves, all beautifully finished, hemmed and lined, and it breaks my heart to think that in subsequent years they have all been lost.

The play was renamed *Belinda And The Baron*, and although I was cast as Belinda, the undoubted star of the show was a little girl called Alfreda Thorogood. Ever the philanthropist, my mother had spotted Freda at my West End dancing classes and offered her and two other girls, a place in our school. Alfreda (we thought it was fun our names being so similar) took the part of the Blackamoor (as it was called then). She brought the house down at every performance and always had to dance an encore. Not surprisingly, Alfreda stayed with ballet all her life, eventually becoming a Prima Ballerina with the Royal Ballet Company, and marrying the wonderful dancer David Wall.

So drama, excitement and lack of what was considered 'normal' teaching, created well-rounded, confident children with a wide span of knowledge and a thirst for more. Success with exams ensured my mother gained a reputation for passing on bright, inquisitive girls to their senior schools. We had the most wonderful teaching staff, including Miss Lavinia Keppel (Mrs Richard Beaumont) who after she finally left LES became governess to Prince Charles and Princess Anne and their cousins. Mrs Helen Wakeford was the best Headmistress and along with Lady Joan Gordon (daughter of the famous General Wavell), Val Mason (niece of James Mason) and several other talented teachers, the team was complete.

My mother was recognised as an authority on education. An avid reader, she learned from those far wiser than her, including Rudolph Steiner. In 1955, when I was fifteen, I accompanied her to the USA on one of her lecture tours there. She was interviewed for magazine articles and her opinion was widely sought. I think the Americans were a little surprised when she likened children to puppies. She said they should have firm boundaries while they were growing up, because although like puppies in a yard they might scrabble at the fences to escape, if they were allowed all the freedom in the world, they would soon become lost. Good discipline was an essential part of her ethos.

My father, a man of sound education and letters, once commented to me, "Your mother is the most uneducated headmistress in England!" Be that as it may, it did not stop her being offered the headship of a very well-known girl's public school.

Somehow I survived being my mother's daughter at Lady Eden's. Luckily I so loved Miss Hayes and my ballet lessons that these years were bearable. I did not enjoy having my mother as Principal though. Mummy would sweep into the assembly hall every morning with her three miniature poodles in tow, to lead the hymns and prayers. Marks were given every week, and I dreaded not coming first as I would receive a reproachful look.

I hated Open Day, as I had no one to whom I could show my work. My Aunt Meme took pity on me once, but she was a bit surprised when she saw the 'embroidered lace handkerchief' that was the result of our needlework classes. Mummy was a brilliant seamstress and her needlework was immaculate. I did not follow in her footsteps. I could not get the wretched handkerchief to look square. The hemming was diabolical, and in the end I became so fed up trying to stitch the lace on that I glued it with runny glue. I gave up trying to embroider a neat little initial, so I drew it on instead with a blue pencil. I didn't think anyone else would see it – but on this occasion I was wrong!

Lady Eden's School continued for many years, and I was honoured to be invited to give the speech at the 50th Anniversary Speech Day in 1997 which was held in the Kensington Town Hall. My brother John and his wife, Margaret Ann were the chatelaines at this time. I like to think my mother was looking down from on high with pride at how her school had succeeded against all odds. Uneducated though she may have been, she was also innovative, brave , talented and above all she had an enormous love for children.

★ ★ ★

As Lady Eden's School in London grew, it became apparent that the children needed a school to which to progress. My parents decided once again to start a school in our house in the New Forest. Several pupils from the London school did indeed progress to Fritham, although the majority of pupils came from elsewhere.

My father was a dominant figure at Fritham House School. He felt that to be truly educated a young woman should be knowledgeable in English, Literature and Language, History, Scripture, Mathematics and at least one if not two foreign languages. He felt that Science was quite unimportant for the average girl, but instead his pupils had a vast knowledge of History of Art and studied not only the greatest painters, sculptors and architects, but also the finest makers of furniture and silver. Fritham House girls could read the hallmarks on silver, and tell the difference between a Chippendale chair and a Hepplewhite.

My mother indulged in her talent of sewing, and taught the girls to make unusual and beautiful objects, most especially christening robes for their future babies! Walks in the forest with Daddy were an education in themselves. Trees and flora and fauna were studied and enjoyed.

Drama was extremely important. Plays were read, studied and performed. Music – the appreciation and playing of instruments - was high on the list. General knowledge was essential, and each year my father produced a general knowledge paper which everyone entered under a pseudonym, only putting their ages on the paper as a guide. Painters were helped and encouraged, and one pupil, Christina Fairweather, became a celebrated artist in her own right, having studied with my father.

Dormitories were pretty, with wallpaper and bedspreads.

Names like The Star, the Circus, Rose and Daffodil – gave a hint to their décor.

Children who wanted to could ride in the forest. Games, especially tennis (five grass and two hard courts) were very important. Pupils, like his own children, would crowd into the library to hear Sir Timothy read the next instalment of a thrilling book.

The school ran in this wonderfully unique way until the death of my father in 1963. My mother then struggled to run both schools, dividing her time between London and the New Forest. She was always exhausted, and never had enough time for anything. I recently found a poignant letter from me, begging her to slow down and take care of herself.

Proud though I was of both schools, I also hated the intrusion on my life. To go 'home' to the New Forest for a weekend during term time was miserable. A member of the staff slept in MY room. I had to sleep in a dormitory with girls I didn't know. I ate in the school dining room, and certain members of the staff took great pleasure in castigating me for minor offences. "Elfrida Eden – do NOT run! Do NOT talk! Do NOT use that staircase!" and so on. It seemed I couldn't escape the schools and bells ordered my life. I yearned for the holidays.

My eldest sister Ann eventually moved into Fritham House with her family and continued to run the school very successfully for many more years. Eventually it was accepted that in this modern age to have a school like Fritham House was no longer viable, and so finally the last pupils left for ever. The FOGS still meet for reunions and those old girls I have met in ensuing years, all look back on their time at Fritham with enchantment and gratitude, combined with love for my parents.

CHAPTER SIX

MY TEACHERS

Violet Ballantyne was small, with jet-black hair which was usually kept off her face with a hair ribbon. Her name was perfect for her. Miss Ballantyne wore ballerina length dresses in pastel colours which had frills at the shoulders and hem, and wide ribbon sashes. On her feet were gold or silver sandals. We all adored her, and when she asked us "What do I like better than good dancing?" we would all reply, "Good manners, Miss Ballantyne". "Be careful children" she would say, "I am on the warpath today!" and we would all pretend to be really scared.

From the ages of five to eight I went almost every day, and the limbering classes were almost as favoured as ballet. Boys joined us for ballroom lessons, which were also fun. The girls would sit straight-backed on gold chairs, ankles neatly crossed and hands demurely in laps. The boys would then enter the room and come up to us, bow, and ask us to dance. We were always taught to say "yes" no matter who asked us, and thence we would begin to learn the foxtrot, the waltz and the quickstep.

It wasn't long before I was one of Miss B's little 'stars'. My mother endlessly stitched yards of net to make my tutus, and I just LOVED being the centre of attention and dancing my heart out. There were several other talented pupils in the classes, the most notable being Anna Massey, who became a famous actress. I appeared in all the shows and discovered how much I enjoyed being on stage. I began to believe that I was without doubt a wonderful dancer. Little did I know my confidence was soon to take a serious pounding.

I was eight years old when my mother announced "Tonight I am taking you with me to a grown-up party. Whoever I introduce you to, be sure to look into their eyes, smile, and be yourself."

What a strange turn of events! Never before had I been allowed to attend a grown-up party, and so wearing my very best dress, and with Mummy's instructions firmly lodged in my ear, I entered a room full of loudly chattering and laughing people, all of whom were complete strangers to me.

"This is my daughter Elfrida" I heard my mother say. I looked up to see an old woman with a kind face. I gazed fixedly into her eyes, smiled my widest smile and said "How do you do", performing a demure little curtsey.

"Charming" murmured the old woman, "So you want to be a ballet dancer, I hear. Then of course I shall introduce you to Anton."

Anton turned out to be the dancer Anton Dolin, who was

at the height of his fame, regularly appearing with his partner Alicia Markova at the Royal Opera House in Covent Garden. Poor Mr Dolin must have wondered why this extraordinary child who rigidly stared into his eyes with a wide, almost manic smile on her face, was being introduced to him at all. "Ohmygod" he probably thought "another pushy mother who thinks her little twinkletoes has talent enough to become a ballerina."

"If your daughter wants to dance" said Anton Dolin to my mother, "She must go to good teachers. The best in London is Madame Vera Volkova. You may bring your daughter to watch my lesson tomorrow, and Madame will have a look at her to see if she has any talent."

I later learned that that kindly old woman was a Russian princess. "She didn't look much like a princess" I said, with a hint of disappointment in my voice.

"The princess is a White Russian," my mother replied, by way of explanation. "She managed to escape." I had no clue as to what she was talking about, and I mildly wondered what other colours the Russians came in.

Sitting on the small stage by the piano in a large but somewhat down-at-heel studio in West Street off Cambridge Circus, I watched with amazement as Madame Volkova gave a lesson to Anton Dolin. I suddenly felt very unsure of myself. The little star of Miss Ballantyne's shows, sweetly prancing about in an Alice blue gown, seemed to bear no relation to the difficult and fascinating class I was watching.

When the lesson was over Mr Dolin introduced me to Madame, and she then made me dance for her. She examined me critically to see if I was the right shape before announcing, "I will accept her as a pupil, but only in the children's classes, which will be taken by my assistant, Peggy Ayres."

So started a new phase of my ballet training. A professional phase. Gone were the luxurious surroundings of Hans Place with its ornate mirrors, gold chairs and the ever-present attentions of nannies. Now I was learning with children from quite a different background to me. Should I ever step out of line or behave in any way as if I was superior to them, I was soon firmly put in my place.

The strange thing was that I loved it. I adored the lessons with Peggy, and worked my very hardest. If anything I sometimes tried too hard, as when I attempted my first pirouette. I used so much energy that I ended up sprawled all over the floor, much to everyone's amusement.

It was at these classes that I first met Alfreda Thorogood. Alfreda's mother played the piano for our lessons, and her lovely sister Pat was already in the Sadler's Wells Ballet Company.

My hard work paid off, and I had progressed to the adult class by the time I was ten. Naturally I was in the back row, but in the front row I would often gaze in awe at the famous dancers of the day. Violetta Elvin, Svetlana Beriosova, John Gilpin and the top stars, Margot Fonteyn and Robert Helpmann, all came to study with the gifted Madame Volkova. I could not believe I was actually allowed to be in the same class as these wonderful dancers. I watched and learned as much as I possibly could.

I am not quite sure how it happened, but one day I found myself sitting in the stalls of an empty Royal Opera House watching Madame coach Margot Fonteyn in a solo dance. I was mesmerised. The stage was enormous and rather bleak looking, with only colourless working lights to brighten it up. Margot was in a tutu, but she also wore a crossover cardigan and leg warmers. She listened intently to her instructions. Suddenly Volkova remembered me, and indicated I should go up on the stage through the pass door.

Was I dreaming? There I was on the stage of the Royal Opera House, Covent Garden, with Margot Fonteyn! I looked at the huge auditorium, all red and gold, and imagined that one day those seats would be filled with a cheering audience, enthusiastically applauding me as I made my humble, but deeply satisfied curtseys. Completely carried away, I duly sank into a deep curtsey – and from the back of the stalls came the sound of one pair of hands clapping, as a cleaner was sweet enough to share in my fantasy!

Vera Volkova had been forced to flee Russia after the revolution. With her friend George Goncharov she ended up in Shanghai, where they not only performed together regularly but started teaching. Amongst their first pupils were the future stars of the Royal Ballet Company Margot Fonteyn and June Brae.

Volkova was considered one of the greatest teachers in the history of ballet, along with Maestro Enrico Cecchetti and Vaganova, under whom she herself had studied. Sadly she was not given the recognition she deserved in England, and she was enticed away by the Royal Danish Ballet Company, which had a tremendous reputation at that time. My mother and I were so sad when she left, as by this time we were firm friends.

Madame's old dancing partner, George Goncharov, took over her ballet studio in West Street. This man became not only my teacher but my mentor and my dearest friend. We called him Gonchi. He would take me to see Russian cartoon films, and then he'd tell me about his beautiful St. Petersburg. His eyes would fill with tears as he described the hot summers lazing on the banks of the Neva, or riding on troikas through the deep snow in the winter months.

Throughout my fractured school days at Lady Eden's, The Arts Educational School, governess at home and boarding at

Heathfield, I continued my lessons with Gonchi. I often had two lessons a day, and would take myself off to the Café Suisse in Soho for a snack at lunch time. Gonchi would join me whenever he could, and I loved to hear his stories of the homeland he missed so much.

One day I was in the café when a group of Russians came in. They noticed me there alone, and the proprietor explained that I was training to dance with Goncharov. "Come here, darlink," one of them said. "Oh she has good legs – but I think she may grow too tall."

Too tall? This was the first time this doubt had entered my mind. It had never occurred to me that I would be too tall, as the rest of my family, apart from my father and Ann, were not the least bit tall.

During my time at boarding school I would come to London twice a week for a private lesson. Immediately after this was finished Gonchi took an advanced ballet class. Quite often the great Robert Helpmann would attend these classes. When he did so he would arrive a bit early in order to allow me to do some 'pas de deux' with him. Sitting on the shoulder of this famous dancer, and then plunging into a fish dive, I felt every inch the ballerina I felt sure I would one day be.

After I had been studying with Gonchi for about four years, I began to notice that he was losing weight. He still banged his stick and shouted at me if I didn't perform to his liking. He still called me his 'little monkey' in Russian, but I knew something was terribly wrong. The blue cardigan that once stretched over a bit too large tummy, now went twice round his waist. One day he hugged me sadly and told me he was very ill. I was fourteen years old and had never known anyone to be seriously ill before. I could not take it in.

I had been asked to perform a solo in a forthcoming charity matinee. Gonchi had created a charming dance for me and we had been working hard to perfect this. The brilliant Clarice Chater was making a deep blue and red tutu especially for this occasion, which was perfect for this rather coquettish dance.

The tutu was not ready when Mummy told me that we were going to visit Gonchi in hospital, and I was to wear my costume for him to see. "But it's not ready" I wailed. "Never mind" said my mother, "you can wear another one." I didn't want to wear the one she chose. It wasn't right for the dance. Added to which I felt an idiot dressed in a ballet costume walking through the hospital.

I was shocked when I saw my Gonchi lying so pale and thin in his hospital bed. My mother said "Here's Elfie. She is in her costume." Gonchi opened his eyes and said, "It should be a tutu. It is not right." With that his eyes closed again, and I was devastated. I wished I hadn't been in a costume at all. I left the hospital in tears, and my darling Gonchi died two days later.

I will never forget how kind my father was to me after Gonchi's death. He was so comforting, and yet it must have been strange for him knowing how much I had loved this man.

A wonderful funeral service was held for him at St Martin in the Fields, and as his coffin entered the church the organist played the haunting scene from *Swan Lake*. Violetta Elvin gave a moving address to the large congregation, ending with the words "Prayshay Georgi". As the doors of the church opened for the coffin to leave we were all amazed to see that during the service there had been a heavy fall of snow, and dearest Gonchi left us in the wintry weather that would have given him such happy memories of his beloved homeland.

★ ★ ★

My mother was extraordinarily particular about my clothes. In fact at times she made my life downright miserable through her obsession.

Mummy had made most of my clothes when I was small as she was brilliant with the needle, executing tiny, even, neat stitches that I could only dream about. Each little dress or pinafore was trimmed with lace, ribbons or broderie anglaise. Mama gloated with pride when people commented on how 'pretty' I looked. This was especially so, as I was indeed her plainest child.

As I grew older I wore bought clothes, and my favourite outfit when I was about seven years old was a little white skirt with matching jacket. I felt so proud and grown-up wearing this, and there is a photograph of me holding a godchild of my mother's at his christening, with Mummy's ever-present hand hovering anxiously in case I dropped the baby.

Part of this favourite suit was alas about to bring me great unhappiness. A little girl called Theodora attended our London school. She was the stepdaughter of the famous actor and matinee idol Jack Buchanan. He was a lovely man, and SO handsome. We were allowed to call him the family's pet name of "Johnny B".

I will never forget Theo's birthday party, which was held in their beautiful apartment in Knightsbridge. Johnny B taught us some fun party tricks, and years later I taught my own offspring these tricks, and subsequently their children as well, where they were equally well received.

Theo was staying with us in the New Forest when the *Queen Elizabeth* sailed into Southampton after a voyage from

New York. Johnny B and his glamorous wife Suzy were on board, and Johnny had invited my mother, Theo and me to have lunch on board ship before they disembarked. I was over the moon with excitement at the thought of actually being on this great ship. I rushed upstairs to lay out my precious white suit on my bed. When the time came to change I was horrified to see the white skirt had been replaced with a pair of RED SHORTS! To make matters worse, the shorts had straps and a BIB. As if this wasn't bad enough Mummy insisted I wore them back to front, so the bib was incongruously at my back.

With a ghastly frilly blouse and red shoes to put on as well, I quickly dissolved into tantrum mode. I shouted and screamed, and refused to put on the shorts. I ran away and hid, and could hear Amelia, of all people, begging Mummy to allow me to wear the skirt. In the end it was either wear the shorts or not go. So, enviously looking at Theo in her little navy suit, I sniffled my way into the car.

Oh how embarrassed and stupid I felt as I walked up the gangplank and stepped inside the mighty liner. I felt sure everybody was looking at this silly little girl in her absurd clothes, topped off by a blotchy face and straight brown hair!

When I was about seven years old my mother looked at me sadly and said I was "shabby". Times were very hard after the war, but I wasn't conscious of being shabby, so I was not unduly concerned. There was enough money however for a great treat. We went to the cinema to see a film starring the American child actress called Margaret O'Brien. This coincided with a visit to London by this little star and my mother heard she was selling some of her clothes.

I was amazed and thrilled when Mummy suddenly appeared carrying several packages which turned out to be wonderful

American clothes. One garment was a grey cape with hood, which was unusual in those days. Mummy was so delighted with this purchase that she took me to a photographer, who proceeded to shoot a series of Polyfotos of me. I had never posed for photographs before and I thoroughly enjoyed the experience. The results were good, although when I look at them today, I am amazed at how Chinese I looked. Mummy also used to call me her little Chinky, and years later, a very eminent and erudite friend of my father's, Sir John Balfour, never called me anything else other than Chink. Sir John Balfour GCMG GBE had met my father in the internment camp at Ruhleben. After the war he was a successful diplomat. He and I formed a friendship I treasure to this day.

My mother was 'in love' with the USA, which surely stemmed from her American heritage. Returning from one of her visits, she presented me with a variety of different coloured ballet costumes, tights and practice skirts. All I had worn until then were somewhat shapeless cotton leotards or tunics in black or white. What a treat! Off I went to my dancing class in the West End proudly wearing my bright new clothes, only to immediately want to remove them, as the other students accused me of showing off. The lovely colours then remained unworn, as I would only put on the black set. Many years later these clothes came into their own as parts of costumes in one of my ballet shows.

Nowadays we are all so spoilt for choice in our clothes. We can choose any colour or style, and on the whole they are not outlandishly expensive. So soon after the war choice was very limited, and the clothes were dull and utilitarian. It was the lucky child who actually had some brand new clothes as opposed to the 'hand-me-downs' and 'make-do-and-mend' variety. To dress in fashion or in the latest 'must have' trend was completely unheard of. Clothes had a function, and that was to cover one's body for all sorts of occasions, and that was all.

I have horrendous memories of shapeless swimsuits – liberty bodices – gaiters and then scratchy woollen leggings. Hats were an important part of all wardrobes, and children as well as adults wore hats, berets, caps or balaclavas as a matter of course. My mother loved her hats, and I recall one of which she was very proud which featured a flying bird in all its glory!

★ ★ ★

Lady Eden's end of term in 1950 was held as usual in our main hall. My mother presided over the event, announcing the names of the children who had passed their Common Entrance Examinations.

"Elfrida Eden passed into Francis Holland and the Arts Educational School," she said, and to amused laughter, "and nobody was more surprised than her mother!" Considering I had been consistently first or second in term order all year, I was somewhat put out at that.

It was decided that I should attend the Arts Educational School (AES) so I could concentrate on my ballet training. Little did I know what I was in for. What a shock awaited me! I had been nurtured in LES, making a curtsey to the teachers, wearing long white socks, sailor dresses, boaters with little white gloves in the summer. I was used to polite, kind children whose childish quarrels were soon over. Now, Wham! Bang! I was thrust into the world of the professional theatrical child, tough, ambitious and cruel.

I might have made it if I had been left alone, as I did have dancing talent and in places like AES talent will always be recognised and respected. But I had my mother. First of all she insisted that I would ONLY do ballet classes and Greek dancing, no tap, modern, character or jazz. During the times my form was attending these classes I was to do extra ballet and acting with older pupils. These advanced students hated me, and quite rightly thought it was absurd that I had been bumped up into their classes, so they went out of their way to make me feel a fool and totally inadequate.

My mother hated the uniform, but won permission for me to wear long white socks instead of the usual grey. Hard to believe now, but long white socks were almost unheard of then, and they gave great cause for mockery, especially amongst the boy pupils. AES was co-ed and this was my first exposure to boys on such a scale.

My mother arranged for me to be given a lift to the school every morning with the father of a child at LES. This man just happened to be the US Ambassador. My lift was in a huge chauffeur-driven Cadillac, and after dropping off the Ambassador at Grosvenor Square I was driven in style to school.

Eventually the mockery and teasing I suffered at this grand arrival every day forced me to beg the driver to let me out around the corner so I could appear to have walked to school like everyone else.

Nowadays I would have told everyone how miserable my life was at AES because of the bullying, but in those days I just had to 'take it on the chin'. The boys would lie in wait for me in the corridors, trip me up as I went by laughing and call me 'White Socks' and 'Miss Fancy Pants'. The older pupils in the drama classes would purposely make me feel small and inadequate, as it was all too obvious I was out of my depth. I held my own in the ballet classes at least, but it didn't really help. Every morning I would awake with a sick feeling in my stomach, knowing I had to go to school.

My ballet classes, however, were not restricted to school. I was allowed (thanks to Mummy) to leave school early twice a week for lessons with Gonchi, where for a few hours I could forget the miseries of school.

On one never-to-be-forgotten occasion, I arrived home quite late and very tired. After supper I settled down to my homework, which was writing a composition. This I enjoyed, and I was just starting when Mummy appeared and ordered me to go to bed at once.

"But my homework!" I wailed.

"Don't worry," said Mama, "I will write it for you". Alarm bells should have rung, but I was tired, and duly went to bed blissfully unaware of what lay ahead.

The following morning I asked for 'my' composition. I could not believe my eyes at what I saw. It was the worst bit of writing ever. Not only was the content totally banal and way below my capabilities, but the actual writing and spelling were both atrocious. My mother had assumed I would misspell almost every work, and she obviously had not checked my book to see my previous work, which was quite well written and for which I had received some good marks.

Silly little me. I took it to school in the grand Cadillac, without thinking that maybe I should lie and pretend I had left it at home, and quickly write another edition that evening. So conditioned was I to obeying that I duly laid it on the teacher's desk, and waited.

"ELFRIDA EDEN!" one of my favourite teachers barked out with uncharacteristic harshness. "STAND UP!" (sniggers and gleeful nudges and winks from my class mates) "NEVER IN MY LIFE HAVE I HAD SUCH AN APPALLING PIECE OF WORK HANDED INTO ME!" continued my teacher, still shouting. Then, in a softer tone, "in fact, it is SO bad and SO unlike anything else you have written, I am wondering if in fact it was you who wrote it. WAS it you who wrote it?"

"No" I replied.

"Then who did?"

Brought up as I had been never to lie, I whispered, "My mother".

"YOUR WHAT?" yelled the teacher, and then a little bit of sense finally came to me. "My brother" I said, a little bit louder. "Oh" said Miss X, "For a minute there I thought you had said your mother!" She calmed down and gave me the opportunity to re-write the essay.

During my time at AES a successful play was running in London which was called *The Bad Seed*. It was a spooky play about two outwardly angelic children who killed their governess. The two girls who shared the lead were in my class, and one of them, Carol Wolveridge, ended up, many years later, working for me as a teacher in my school. How I wish I had known that then!

Mummy finally realised how unhappy I was, and as I suspect AES found it difficult having a pupil who demanded so many special arrangements, it was mutually agreed that I should leave. Looking back, I realised I missed many lovely opportunities, as I grew to love tap, modern, character and especially jazz dancing. Because of my height, it would have been wise to have let me study all forms of dancing, but darling mama wanted classical ballet, or nothing.

★ ★ ★

When I left the hated Arts Educational School in 1951, it was decided that I should stay at home for a while and be taught by a governess. In this way my ballet classes could be easily accommodated. Mrs Beaumont entered my life, and what a joy she was!

My bedroom was transformed into a school room, and Mrs B and I were happy as Larry working together. I adored her lessons in history (especially French history), literature and English. I enjoyed French, and didn't mind geography. I loathed and detested maths, but Mrs B was such a dear, as I think she hated this subject as much as I did, so we just whizzed over a few sums before returning to reciting Shakespeare or learning about the French Revolution.

Mary Hayes, now Lady Bethune, was still a very important member of Lady Eden's School. With Mary (as I was now allowed to call her), I studied poetry. We used to sit in the drawing room of Victoria Road reading poetry to each other with huge passion, enjoyment, and sometimes floods of tears when reading a poem like *Beth Gelert*. This was the tragic tale of the huntsman Llewellyn, who stabbed his favourite hound to death when he thought the dog had killed his baby son, but then discovered, too late, that Beth Gelert had valiantly fought and defeated a fearsome wolf that had tried to attack the baby, who was unharmed. This is a true story, and I can still cry when reading the poem.

I will ignore another Miss B, who managed to kill my enjoyment of learning to play the piano, and instead dwell on the happy memories of the other two Bs, Beaumont and Bethune, and then another superb ballet teacher who had replaced Peggy a year earlier. Enid (who was married to Gordon Murray, the creator of *Trumpton* for the BBC) had studied with equally famous Russians, which meant she was quite unlike the usual English ballet teacher, and she was also marvellously theatrical and flamboyant.

LES was growing apace and had expanded into the next door house, no 41. We lived on two floors and the school had the rest. My life was still governed by bells, but apart from that, this was indeed a wonderfully happy time of my life. Mummy almost ruined it by insisting I wore the equivalent of the school uniform pinafore, only in bright red or blue. I had to eat with the little children, and felt a fool in my voluminous garment when in reality I was an 'old' girl, and almost completely grown up!

My spoiling time at home did not last. My father now insisted that I should go to a boarding school to be properly educated.

CHAPTER SEVEN

SCRAPES AND JAPES

As a little girl I devoured schoolgirl stories, especially those by Enid Blyton and Angela Brazil. The former author I was forbidden to read by my father ("Trash!") so I put A. Brazil dust covers on the wicked books I was not allowed.

I longed to be a real schoolgirl, getting into frightful scrapes, having midnight feasts and pillow fights and enjoying wicked pranks and jolly japes. Most of all I longed to wear a navy blue tunic and tie, complete with navy blue knickers. I was somewhat disappointed to see that Heathfield, the school my parents chose for me, had no tunics. However, there was quite a lot of navy blue, complete with tie AND knickers (though these were mainly worn during games).

My mother knew the headmistress, a lovely woman called Miss Dodds. I can see them now, my mother and Miss Dodds walking arm in arm, because – I might have guessed it – Mummy had made special arrangements for me to be different. First of all I was not allowed to play games. I found this dreadfully hard, and so longed to play lacrosse and rounders. I had quite a good eye for the ball, and thanks to my dancing training, I was quick and light on my feet. I persuaded the girls to teach me in break, and was invited to play rounders for my house, but not for the school. Not playing games, not being part of a team, immediately set me apart and made me an 'oddball' once again.

The school raincoat was navy, but I had had a new grey one for AES, so I was allowed to wear that. I stood out like a sore thumb when we walked in crocodile on wet days.

For the summer term the school gave us a choice of dresses to have made. Gingham material in four alternative colours could be selected, and they suggested a choice of three patterns. They had reckoned without my mother, who took one look at the patterns and decided they were far too plain for me. She chose to make my dresses herself. Instead of the perfectly acceptable desired patterns, my dresses were trimmed with little bits of lace and tucked here and there to give them 'shape', with very full skirts that were made to be worn over petticoats. Of course I never wore the petticoats as they weren't on the list, but try as I might, I could not make these dresses seems 'ordinary'.

The games mistress loathed me. She could not understand why I did not play games, so she set out to make my life a misery – and she succeeded. Her best moment came at the beginning of the second term, when we all had our trunks unpacked and checked by a member of staff. Just my luck to have Miss B. "Oh my goodness!" Miss B. said at the top of her voice, thereby ensuring she had the full attention of everyone in the dormitory. "The school list says you must have six pairs of white cotton underpants. Now – let me see – here I have one, two and three pairs of white frilly, lacy, NYLON underpants. Oh look" she continued, "I have found one, two and three pairs of PINK frilly, lacy NYLON underpants. Mmm, that makes six pairs. Are you wearing any pants today, Elfrida?" (stifled giggles from my fellow pupils) "Yes Miss B." I replied, "And pray - do tell us – what colour are they?" I did it again – still the idiot and conditioned to telling the truth. "Pale blue" I whispered, whereupon the rest of the dormitory collapsed in a heap of giggles.

Despite these setbacks I enjoyed my time at Heathfield and made good friends, some of whom I have to this day. Unlike the cruelty of the children at AES, where I was mercilessly mocked and humiliated, my new schoolmates coped with my oddness.

My main oddity was my ballet training. Twice a week my dear teacher Enid came to the school to teach me. Enid was an inspirational teacher, and in her way quite eccentric. Her theatricality was a bit too much at times, but I didn't mind. Enid taught me to 'perform', as she herself had been taught by brilliant Russian teachers.

I had my lessons in a room where there was a window in the door. Time and again I would see girls peering through this glass and convulsing themselves with laughter at Enid's 'over the top' demonstrations.

Twice a week I went to London for lessons with Goncharov. To get to London I had to go by train – on my own. I was thirteen years old and Mummy was convinced I would be kidnapped, so she arranged with the stationmaster at Ascot

Station to allow me to travel with the guard in the guard's van!
The guard's van had no seating, no heating and no light. I was
alone for the fifty-minute journey with an unknown man. Very
safe!

Because it was often cold, I had to wear a huge grey duffle
coat, and I also carried a little fold-up stool to use as a seat. While
I was waiting for the taxi to take me to the station, I used to
pray that no child would come by and see me, but they did,
often. "What are YOU doing sitting there and why are you in
that big coat and with a stool?" they would say. With some
imagination I could have concocted some elaborate reason for
all this, but instead, as usual, I told the truth. "The GUARD'S
van?" would be the incredulous retort, "but WHY?"

I was extremely lucky. The guard was a nice man. Eventually
he felt sorry for me sitting on my beastly little stool, so he invited
me to the far more comfortable position of sitting on his lap! I
enjoyed looking through his periscope and seeing our train
snaking away before us. I felt quite at ease on his lap, and no
alarm bells rang. Finally I told my mother – and she freaked!
Another visit to the stationmaster ensued, and this resulted into
my being locked inside a Ladies' Only carriage.

These trains had no corridors, and many women travelling
alone wanted to be in a single sex carriage. I would sit at each
station hoping and praying no one would try to come in. They
always did, and they were always furious. They banged on the
door and yelled at the guard, while I sat inside cringing with
humiliation. I did think once it might be quite fun to put on a
really 'mad' act, but I lacked the courage.

On arrival at Waterloo the guard would unlock the crazy
child, and I would rush to the barrier, where Mummy would
be waiting. Then we would be driven to West Street in great

splendour, as Mummy always hired a limousine from Queensberry Hire, and she and I sat in the back while I ate the sandwiches that had been lovingly prepared for me by our cook. The grand limousine and chauffeur looked somewhat out of place in grubby West Street, but I didn't mind, as the best part of the day now started. I dashed upstairs to the studio, for my lesson with Gonchi. Mama would watch and take notes.

My journeys back to school were fine. They were normal. Mummy and I had made friends with a lovely girl who attended a course in London daily, and she took the same train as I did. I sat with her and chatted away happily, relishing the experience of just being ordinary. On Wednesdays, my extra treat was to get my two comics, *Girl* and *School Friend*, which was utter heaven!

I certainly had my fair share of midnight feasts and pillow fights at Heathfield. I loved it all. I held my own scholastically in all subjects but one. I was a year ahead in French, so that was no problem, and the geography and history teachers liked me as I used the library for reference, and could draw maps neatly. I loved literature and English, but the hows, the whys and the wherefores of maths (algebra – geometry – basic arithmetic) completely mystified me. The maths teacher despaired of me, but she was kind enough once to give me three marks out of one hundred for an algebra exam. These marks were for neatness, as every single thing I had put down was wrong!

Typical of my parents, they decided after one year to remove me from Heathfield. The new plan was to attend a tutorial college in London in the afternoons, and leave me free to dance all morning.

Before I left the school, I gave a ballet performance. I wore my beautiful pink tutu, which had been so expertly created for me by Clarice Chater. (Why oh why were these wonderful costumes not kept for me?) The sniggering girls who had peered through the window during my lessons were gratifyingly stunned into silence and then there came a huge round of applause and cheering. The memory will stay with me as one of my most satisfying performances.

I enjoyed being in the school chapel, and I wept buckets at my leaving service. I could not believe I was going when I was just beginning to cement my friendships. On the train journey back to London with the other children, I threw my boater out of the window as tradition demanded. My mother was not amused.

* * *

By the time I left Heathfield I had attended Miss Ironside's School, the Lycée Francais, Lady Eden's School and the Arts Educational School and had had my governess. I was now about to attend my final seat of learning – Miss Dixon and Miss Wolfe, in Victoria Street, London. Miss Dixon and Miss Wolfe, known to all and sundry as the Wolfe and the Vixen, ran a tutorial college for oddballs like me.

I studied only four subjects, French, History, English and English Literature. Maths was a thing of the past, and somehow I have got through life without it, but with a rather good 'sixth sense' when I'm spending too much money.

Darling Gonchi had died during the Christmas holidays and now every morning I went to my new ballet teacher, a wonderful Russian woman called Cleo Nordi, for class, after which I caught a bus to Victoria for afternoon school lessons. Three times a week, I then returned to Nordi for another class before going home to do my homework and flop into bed.

I also had private 'pas de deux' lessons with another Russian called Zeglovski. He was not at like Gonchi, and while he was, I am sure, a superb teacher, he unnerved me when we danced the romantic 'pas de deux' dances from *Swan Lake, Don Quixote* or *Romeo and Juliet*.

This was quite a tough schedule for a fourteen-year-old who was still, unfortunately, growing, but somehow I also managed to find time to teach the pupils at the school a short ballet I had created and subsequently entered in a competition for choreography. For the same event Enid had taught me a very difficult dance from *Coppélia* called *Prayer*. After the competition had taken place we were very happy to be notified that both numbers received gold medals, and I was invited to perform *Prayer* in the finals of the competition.

As the date of the finals approached I became increasingly nervous, as it was apparent that children from all over the UK were taking part. My mother was unfazed and utterly convinced I would win. She even talked about "When Elfie wins…" and no amount of protestations from me had any effect on her. I was thinking about the many talented and professional children I had come across at the Arts Educational School, and knew I would have tough competition.

On the day itself my mother had invited several friends to come and watch my triumph. I wished she hadn't. I wanted to keep everything quiet. My sister Rose agreed to accompany me on the piano, which was brave of her as the score is very hard, but she played it faultlessly.

At the theatre I sat in my costume, in the auditorium watching the other dances, knowing I had plenty of time to warm up before my turn. Suddenly someone appeared at my side and said, "Quick – you are on next – two candidates have dropped out and you are to go now."

This was NOT good preparation for *Prayer,* which unsurprisingly is a slow dance requiring deep concentration and perfect balance 'sur les pointes'. With downcast eyes I rose up on my 'pointes' and began my tiny 'bourrées' onto the stage.

"Joyce – quickly – come here. This looks as if it's going to be good!" The stage whisper from the wings cut through my concentration. I opened my eyes and immediately saw the row of adjudicators hunched over their low lights, pens poised, looking straight back at me. I stepped into my first arabesque on point and promptly wobbled. A gasp came from the audience, and I was totally thrown.

I struggled on, but I knew I was lost. I could dance this solo well, but I needed to be 'at one' with the music. I knew I hadn't performed to the best of my ability. As I returned to the auditorium for the rest of the event, I caught my mother's eye. Her look of disappointment, hurt and anger haunted me for years.

Apparently I was placed second. Second, alas, is not the same as winning. The girl who won had performed a bright, fast number with lots of 'flashy bits' as Enid used to call them.

Part of the first prize was to be invited to dance in the National Display of Dancing at the Royal Albert Hall. Despite not winning the competition I was not only invited to take part, but also asked to perform a solo, with the request that this would be *Prayer.* I was told to attend rehearsals at the Italia Conti School the following Saturday, and to show *Prayer* to the organisers. But I knew I could never dance this solo again. The hurt and shame were too raw. "I have another dance," I announced. "I would prefer to do that." I was told to show this as well on Saturday.

I was lying of course, as I had no dance in mind. I had no alternative but to choreograph one myself, as my mother had by this time lost interest and was not inclined to pay for the extra lessons I would need to learn and polish a new dance.

I chose some music I knew well and loved and created a dance. Happily the committee liked it and allowed me to perform it. I naughtily pretended Gonchi had choreographed it, as I knew they would not approve if they realised it had been mine alone.

I so enjoyed preparing for this show, as I also danced in group numbers with many other children who were far more professional than I was. The actual competition winner was in the groups but didn't have a solo. She was understandably put out.

The National Display of Dancing was a huge event. Participants came from all over the country and there was standing room only. The item I was in was called *North, South, East and West*. *North* was a Scottish gentleman, *East* was a Chinese girl, *West* was a cowboy and don't ask me why, but I was *South*. I danced in the vast arena of the hall, in the tutu I should have shown Gonchi when he was dying in hospital. I am sure I was not very good, but it was a great experience. Nobody had been invited to see me this time. I had just turned fifteen years old.

Cleo Nordi was another brilliant teacher. Her class was attended by almost as many men as girls. She held her lessons in the top half of an old church near Olympia. It made a wonderful studio, with its high ceilings.

Cleo was amazing at remembering ballets, and with her I learned many of the famous dances from the classical ballets that are still performed today. Two of my friends also studied with Mme Nordi, and the three of us performed dances from *Les Sylphides* at a charitable performance in front of Dame Ninette de Valois, then head of the Sadler's Wells (later the Royal Ballet) Company and School. After the performance Miss de Valois came on stage, and invited my friend Veronica and me to join the classes at the Senior Ballet School. This was a huge honour and luckily we passed the audition we had to take later and were accepted. Our third dancer, Juliet, was still a little young, although she was a beautiful dancer. Veronica and I went as often as we could to Talgarth Road for lessons, which was particularly pleasing for me as I had failed the audition as a little girl.

Veronica eventually joined the Sadler's Wells Opera Company as a dancer, and there she met, fell in love with and married the famous conductor Sir Alexander Gibson.

GCE exams were looming, and my mother was utterly convinced I would fail them. When the results came through I was at Fritham for the holidays. My dear friend Anna Clamp (Langton) who attended our school in the New Forest, was also there.

Anna's results came before mine, and she passed brilliantly. "Such a good thing hers came first," said dear Mama, "she was bound to pass so well, and as you have probably failed people might not notice now." Oh ye of little faith... I passed all my exams, albeit not brilliantly, but I passed.

During my time at the Wolfe and the Vixen, I had been very excited to have been picked to dance in a new ballet that was being choreographed by a fellow pupil at Nordi's called Donato Forte. After classes were over I would journey to Notting Hill Gate, where we rehearsed in the Rambert School. I was so enjoying the rehearsals with Donato, and loved being part of a 'grown-up' company. Donato had given me a rather special role, and in it I had a pas de deux with a man who was meant to be my lover. It was a very sensuous dance, and I was somewhat embarrassed. I had had no experience with boys whatsoever, and simply didn't know how to project the passion needed for the dance.

Eventually Donato became exasperated with me. He raised his voice and said, "What on earth is the matter with you? You are so wooden. You are sexually attracted to him and you need to show it. Anyone would think you had never had any experience!"

"I haven't" I whispered.

"What?" said Donato. "How old are you for goodness sake?"

The reply of "nearly fifteen" really shocked him. Now he was the one who was embarrassed, and he apologised, and then explained I couldn't stay in the group as I would be too young to perform in public. He had assumed I was older – as people often did – because of my height.

In fact I could have had quite a lot of fun with my height and long legs, if I had been allowed. One day, when I was thirteen and dancing with Gonchi, an elderly woman was watching the class. When it finished, she invited me to be a Bluebell Girl in Paris! I think I really would have enjoyed that, but it was a complete no-no as far as my parents were concerned.

My Uncle Anthony became Prime Minister on May 27th 1955 while I was at Dixon and Wolfe, and along with my friends we toasted his success – with a chocolate!

CHAPTER EIGHT

WHEN LIBERACE
CAME TO TEA

I immediately felt very grown up, having left school at last. I felt sure I would never have to endure another scholastic lesson again. Wrong!

During the immediate aftermath I spent the summer holidays at Fritham, and as usual the days were a mixture of ballet practice, looking after the ponies, walking the dogs and painting school furniture. I returned to London for the term time, and my mother employed me part-time to work in the school. I also attended ballet classes every day at least twice.,

My mother had the habit of rushing into my bedroom in the mornings to say "So and so is ill and can't come in today so you have to take her classes." I became quite adept at teaching all primary school ages in every subject, even maths. My duties also included taking the children for walks in the park, and being on cloakroom duty. I think I was given a little pocket money for all this. The experience however was invaluable, especially for the way my life eventually turned out.

A friend of my mother's called Lady Tarbat decided in September 1956 to start a course for young ladies called 'Social Graces'. She asked my mother if I would mind attending the inaugural course as a publicity student. Mummy and I thought it would be fun – and so it turned out to be.

The course was for three weeks only and took place in the afternoons, so it was possible to do my ballet in the mornings. I really enjoyed myself learning useful things like changing a plug on a lamp, ironing shirts and trousers and beauty tips as well as the (frankly dotty) class on creating little roses out of cherry tomatoes, cream cheese and cochineal. We did flower arranging, we were taught the correct way to introduce people, and we were given guidance on how to buy clothes, including to always sit down and view from the back as well before you buy. I remember much of what I was taught during these three weeks, and am very grateful. I fear however that the courses were not very successful.

On October 9th 1956 we had a great excitement. Liberace was coming to tea! Liberace was a great star. My mother and I would sit in front of our small black and white TV set and watch our favourite programmes. One of these was *I Love Lucy*, starring Lucille Ball, and the other was the *Liberace Show*.

No one had ever seen an entertainer quite like Liberace before. He was, as they say a 'larger than life' character. He played the piano brilliantly, albeit while lacking certain qualities that make a great concert pianist. He was flamboyant. He was razzamatazz. He was 'showbiz'.

Liberace's trademark was the candelabra he placed on his grand piano. We all knew he had a brother called George, and we knew as well that he was a devoted son to his mother. Liberace never seemed to stop smiling, and elderly matrons on both sides of the Atlantic adored him.

The clothes Liberace wore were amazing. Long before Elton John, he was wearing outrageously flashy diamante-studded, feathered, mink-trimmed costumes.

Liberace was coming to England for a series of concerts, but love him as we might have done, it didn't really occur to us to try and get tickets for one of these shows. It was therefore quite a surprise when my mother said to me after his arrival in London, "Liberace is coming to tea with us on Tuesday!"

My brother, John Eden MP, had been asked to show Liberace around the Houses of Parliament. It was then that this famous man said that what he really wanted was to have a proper English tea, with a proper English lady. Despite the fact that no one could accuse my mother of totally fitting this bill, my brother immediately proposed a visit to Victoria Road.

Total panic set in. Because half our house was a school, we really didn't have the set-up to hold a formal tea party. Any silver we had was tucked away in the huge walk-in safe at Fritham. Thankfully the wonderful Mary Bethune had a silver teapot and jug which she lent us. Our drawing room was rearranged to include a tea table, and a patisserie opposite Harrods called Gloriette delivered a selection of dainty sandwiches and cakes. In the meantime I decorated a large piece of paper for Liberace, George and Mom to sign.

The limousines arrived, and the school kitchen staff and

several onlookers were in the road waiting to see this great man. He was huge, and he wore a large overcoat draped over a glinting gold suit. Mom was a sweet little woman who wore an enormous brooch in diamonds and jet of a grand piano.

It was quite one of the funniest occasions I had witnessed, as I saw a side of my mother I had never seen before. She was putting on a brilliant act as the archetypical English hostess, and Mom and George were putty in her hands.

Liberace must have thought we were all quite extraordinary, but he was most gracious, and when I presented him with my piece of paper he took up the whole page with his signature, so there was no room for anyone else.

Liberace's visit coincided with the first-ever visit from the Russian Bolshoi Ballet Company. My friend Veronica, who lived with us at this time, my mother and I were all in a lather of excitement at the prospect of seeing famous Russian dancers we had only heard about. Mummy had managed to get us some good tickets at the Royal Opera House.

For a while the visit of the company was in doubt, as the Russians had invaded Hungary and were committing dreadful atrocities.

On October 6th Mummy and I saw *Swan Lake,* starring Rima Karelskaya. This was the first time I had seen the unique way the Russian ballerinas used their arms. The effect of these almost liquid arms made one think that they must have an extra joint somewhere. English dancers could not replicate this movement.

At this time of my life I was becoming depressed about my great and towering height. I felt HUGE and ungainly, and I began to realise, with bitterness in my heart, that I would never succeed as a classical ballet dancer.

The 12th October is a day I shall forever remember, as I saw Galina Ulanova dance Giselle. Ulanova in those days was as famous as Anna Pavlova had been. Her performance was totally extraordinary, especially her first appearance as a 16-year-old girl. I believe Ulanova was in her forties at the time. Mummy and I were overwhelmed and I feel so lucky that I was able to see her.

Several of us decided to queue for more tickets, and this involved sleeping all night outside the Royal Opera House in Covent Garden. One man took charge, and kept a list of the times everyone had arrived. In this way we could escape for a while and not risk losing our place.

In the early hours of the morning, Veronica and I visited the old Covent Garden Market. This was buzzing with life and activity as farmers from the countryside arrived with their fruit, flowers and vegetables to sell. The scene was pure *My Fair Lady*. Veronica and I had great fun, and we joined the costers for a drink of something between coffee and tea. After this we went to Trafalgar Square, which at that hour was quite deserted. V and I decided to dance round the fountains. What an extraordinary feeling it was, dancing our hearts out under the watchful, one-eyed gaze of Nelson on his column!

We duly got our tickets, although they were standing only. We didn't mind, we just wanted to see whatever we could. My brother John also took me to Croydon to see the Bolshoi when the Covent Garden season was over, and he and I went quite mad clapping and shouting, cheering and stamping feet. By this time I had totally fallen in love with a magnificent male dancer called Nicolai Fadeyechev. He was SO strong and SO masculine and SO handsome. I dreamt about sitting on his shoulders and plunging into my fish dive!

Before the Bolshoi Company left the UK a reception was

given for them at the Russian Embassy in October. My mother, brother and I were invited to attend. My first impression of all the dancers, including the wonderful Ulanova, was how drab and dull they looked. In the centre of a large table which was spread with delicacies, including a mass of caviar, was a huge bowl of fruit which was meant as decoration. These dancers one and all made a beeline for the fruit and were busy chomping on apples and peeling oranges as fast as they get their hands on them.

I saw my divine Nicolai. He was still divine. He spoke no English and I only knew the few words Gonchi had taught me, so in my best ballet mime, I showed him how wonderfully I thought he had danced. In beautiful mime he replied to me. This little exchange was witnessed by their ballet master, who was next to my mother. He asked her if I studied ballet. Mummy told him I had, but sadly I was too tall.

"She would not be too tall in Russia" he said, "send her over to us. I would love to teach her." Mummy and I were tempted. Daddy of course, sensibly would not hear about it. Every day the news from Hungary was worse and undoubtedly it would have been the wrong decision.

On November 3rd 1956, my Uncle Anthony gave an address on the TV and radio about the invasion of Hungary by Russia. I was very proud watching my handsome uncle on this occasion.

★ ★ ★

It was wonderful having Veronica Waggett to live with us, as she and I shared so much. We were both devoted to our ballet and used to dance together at home in the evenings.

When Dame Ninette de Valois had invited us both to attend

classes at the Sadler's Wells School in West London, we would go together as often as possible. For me there was the initial excitement of actually being at this famous school, although there were times when I felt somewhat out of my depth. Teachers such as Pamela May and Harold Turner were wonderful to me, but others were not so kind. At only fifteen I was in a class that was at least three years above me. On the whole I managed quite well, although I could see I lacked strength. V and I went to these classes two or three times a week.

One day we heard that a famous Russian ballerina called Tamara Karsarvina was in London, and would give two open classes. What excitement! Karsarvina had been the mistress of the last Tsar of Russia and she had been his favourite dancer. Somehow she had managed to escape during the revolution in that country. We knew she must be very old, but almost every dancer in London squeezed into the studio to take part in such a unique event.

When Karsarvina entered holding the arm of a young man, I was not alone in wondering what form this lesson would take. Immediately she gave us our first exercises, she came round studying us. She corrected me! Oh the joy – to think I had been touched by this famous dancer who in turn had touched the Tsar of Russia! I treasured the advice and teaching she imparted and subsequently passed on her words to my own students. My abiding memory of this amazing old woman was seeing her lift her leg to an incredible height while executing a '*développer à la seconde*' using the young man as a barre.

In March 1956 we had a good break. With Mummy, V and I went to New York City for a holiday. Naturally we went by sea, and I was utterly delighted to find our ship was to be the *Queen Elizabeth*. This was the ship in which I had had lunch with Jack Buchanan wearing my ridiculous clothes, and Mummy and I had also voyaged on her when I was eleven years old.

Nothing can compare with travelling on a great liner. The almost tangible excitement at the quayside would be replaced by the calm of finally climbing the gangplank, where a senior member of the ship's company would greet each passenger before they were ushered to their cabin. Bon Voyage telegrams and flowers from family and friends combined to ensure a feeling of glamour and elegance that sadly is so lacking in travel today. How lucky we were in those days. No one worried about terrorists. It was assumed that everyone who travelled was who they purported to be, and celebrities were able to relax and unwind for the 5–8 days the Atlantic crossing might take.

Veronica and I immediately explored the ship, and discovered that the gym would be a good place to practise our ballet every day. Somehow it became known we were dancers, and we were persuaded to perform at the farewell concert. After a couple of rough days, we were extremely grateful for a 'millpond' sea.

New York City was electrifying, and my Aunt Phil was delighted to see us. Almost immediately Mummy tried to get us into the NY City Ballet School for a month. In the changing room I met a well-known ballerina called Alexandra Danilova. She wondered who I was, and I told her I had studied with Goncharov and Volkova. She was delighted, as they had all been great friends.

The incredibly famous dancer and choreographer George Balanchine took my first class, and to my horror he put me in the front row. I was terrified, but then immensely proud as he made me execute my '*entrechat six*' alone, as beats and pirouettes were the two things I really could do quite well. However they couldn't fit us in, so we enrolled with the American Theatre Ballet School instead, and thoroughly enjoyed our lessons there.

There was a daily TV programme called *The Clare Mann Show*, and somehow Clare Mann heard about us and wanted us to dance on her show. This we did – on a postage stamp of a floor – and apparently we were liked, so a week later we appeared again, this time with Mummy, who was interviewed about her schools. Clare and my mother then became close friends and stayed in touch until sadly this sweet woman died of cancer.

V and I so enjoyed our time in NY and were miserable at having to leave, although the thought of another voyage on our lovely ship was enticing.

On returning to England I was gradually beginning to accept the awful truth that I might not make the grade as a ballet dancer. I still had at least two lessons a day, and continued with my pas de deux lessons with Zeglovski, even though he pawed me at every opportunity. Poor V was often pressured into coming with me to keep me safe!

I could not imagine my life without ballet. Ever since I had been accepted by Madame Volkova at the age of nine, ballet lessons had dominated my existence. I was hardly ever out of practice, and had lessons during the holidays (at Fritham I would often attend classes in Southampton and Bournemouth). It never occurred to me, or indeed to my mother, that I would not succeed in the end. We tried to ignore my ever-increasing height. Certainly at Sadler's Wells I became very conscious of how tall I had become.

Towards the end of the year during which I had been attending these classes, Ninette de Valois and her entourage arrived to watch our class. This had happened before, so I was not unduly worried, even when I saw Madam looking at me quite often. I just danced my very best. It was therefore a shock when Mummy called me into her room later on that day.

"I have just had a telephone call from Anton Dolin" she told me. "Dame Ninette asked him to pass on the message to you that very sadly she has concluded you are too tall to consider a career in classical ballet."

That was it then. After all those years of training and keeping in practice wherever I was; all the money that had been spent on my lessons; all the joys of successes and the tears of failure, it had all been for nothing.

I felt the bottom had dropped out of my world. I had no purpose in life any more. What could I possibly be if I was not going to be a dancer? My mother's disappointment was as my own, and we both felt bereft.

For days I would awake in tears. I refused to listen to any ballet music. Mummy's hurt manifested itself by completely losing interest. She had wanted my success with all her heart, and she was desolated. In a sense we were grieving. Our grief was for a lost dream.

However I was still only sixteen years old, and if truth be told, I did not really enjoy all the classes I had had at Sadler's Wells. I had found them "awfully English". With the honesty of hindsight, apart from my height, I do not think I was Royal Ballet standard. The emphasis on training by Russian teachers in those days veered towards artistic interpretation, rather than strict technique. Gradually it dawned on me that while nothing would ever kill my love of dancing, I could perhaps still use all my training to good use in another direction.

I then made the decision for myself that I would continue with my classes, but learn other forms of dance as well. How glad I am that I did not give up. To this day, play me some jazz, rock n' roll or Charleston music and you won't be able to keep me down!

There was one occasion years later when I was able to dance in St Petersburg in memory of my darling Gonchi. My husband and I were visiting this glorious city with friends. After a delicious dinner and far too much vodka, I wandered into the lobby of the hotel where we were staying to listen to a talented pianist.

Despite our lack of common language this man understood when I asked him to play the 'scene' from *Swan Lake*. As he played, I started to dance. It was just me and the pianist, or so I thought. Gradually people began to appear and stand silently watching. I was not aware of them until at the end, I received a round of applause, not only from the guests, but from several members of the kitchen staff as well! Gonchi would have been so pleased. I am sure my technique was appalling, but I danced with lots of expression.

CHAPTER NINE

PARIS

At the end of 1956, my parents decided I should live in Paris for a while to learn to speak French properly, and it was agreed that I should still continue with my ballet lessons, as there was a wonderful Russian teacher there called Madame Egorova.

My mother was somewhat nervous at the thought of letting me loose in Paris on my own. However, her fears were somewhat allayed by us having a family friend who lived there, and who took it upon herself to find me suitable lodgings.

Our friend was called Nini, and like my dear friend Veronica, she had lived with us as a member of our family for years while her parents were abroad. Nini's parents were both renowned painters by the name of Guevara and they had the distinction of being the only husband and wife to both have paintings hanging in the Tate Gallery in London at the same time. Nini was like another sister and similar to Amelia in that she was a daredevil and always getting into trouble. It was wonderful to know she was nearby when I went to live in Paris. She found me a room with the Colombier family, and I duly presented myself to them in January 1957.

Their house was within walking distance of the studio of Mme. Egorova in the 9ième district, which as my parents didn't know Paris they assumed was perfectly acceptable. The Colombiers also organized a French tutor for their foreign students, so the whole arrangement sounded ideal.

The house was typically Parisian, with the façade facing the street being occupied by the concierge, a divine old woman called Mlle. Collobert. A passage led one past this apartment and into an inner courtyard, which gave on to the main house. In retrospect it was rather a nice house – and fairly big. It needed to be, as there were quite a few of us living there!

M. and Mme Colombier had three children of their own. Then there was an English girl called Annabel and Dutch girl named Katinka. So far so good. In addition there was a young man called Gérard who was a student at the Military Academy of St. Cyr, and two young men called Jean and Didier. An older Dutch man (about 25) was the remaining resident.

The Colombier family occupied the first two floors and the rest of us slept on the top floor. This was originally an enormous *atelier* which had been divided in two by a curtain. There was also a bit of plywood which did not reach the floor. The boys were one side and the girls the other. Oh, if only my mother had seen this set up!

I was enormously shy my first day, especially when Annabel

insisted on speaking to me only in French. I never forget her "dors bien" as I lay on my bed. Very meanly a month later Annabel's place was taken by Ann, and on her first night I did the same to her. I hope she has forgiven me. In subsequent weeks we became partners in crime, to the despair of Mme. Colombier.

Katinka was huge fun, and the first atheist I had ever come across. She was very worldly wise, and I felt, and knew myself to be, a completely innocent child in her presence.

Out of the door on my first day, I immediately found myself in Place Pigalle. We were right in the centre of Montmartre, and each day, as I walked to Egorova's studio, I had to put up with whistles and cat calls and shouts of "*Bonjour, Double Mètres!*"

Ann and I had great fun exploring Montmartre. We had dreadful portraits drawn for us by impoverished art students. We dutifully toured the Sacré Coeur, but when we emerged from the front door my eyes lusted after the wonderful green grass laid out before us, cascading all down the hill. Memories of rolling down the hills at Fritham came flooding back and I found I was unable to resist the temptation. So upon seeing the green slopes before the Sacré Coeur, nothing could stop me, and soon I was careering down the hills, gathering speed as I went and landing in a heap at the bottom, roaring with laughter. I finally stood up and saw the bemused looks of Parisians and foreign tourists who, when realizing my nationality, nodded to themselves as if to say, "*Certainement, les Anglaises sont vraiment folles!*"

My ballet lessons were a huge success. I loved Mme. Egorova, and got on with my fellow students despite my poor French. One day when executing a '*pirouette sur les pointes*' in class, I found my perfect balance, and instead of the usual double, or if I was lucky triple turn, I did six! I was so amazed I wandered to the side of the class in a trance, only to be called back to finish the sequence. Happily this amazing feat was witnessed by some of the class!

Three days a week we had lessons in the dining room with M. Defarge. He was totally lacking any sense of humour and I fear Ann and I behaved disgracefully. We must have been a nightmare for the poor man, and I doubt I learned much from him, which was a total disgrace.

M. Defarge did take us to museums and art galleries, which on the whole we enjoyed. However, Ann and I always managed to give him the slip when going home, and we took our time stopping off at the Café Suisse to drink gorgeous hot chocolate AND devour an enormous slice of yummy cake. By the time we had walked all the way back to Rue Victor Massé, we were hungry again!

Katinka had won permission – she was older than us – to take us out one evening to visit a friend. This friend was a young man who was living the archetypal existence in a Parisian attic. There was not much space in his room because of his oversized bed, so we all sat on that. It was here, on this and subsequent occasions, that I learned to smoke – *les Disques Bleues*. I coughed and spluttered, but I hung in there, and felt so hugely grown up sharing a bed in an attic in Paris with friends and smoking Gauloise cigarettes.

A strange realization came to me after my first month in Paris. For the first time in my life I was being accepted – liked or disliked – entirely for me and me alone. I was so used to being my mother's daughter or my uncle's niece or my brother's sister that it was a revelation to be just me, and totally liberating.

We weren't bad all the time. Ann loved classical music, though up until then the only classical music I enjoyed was ballet music. I entered our room one evening and Ann was lying on her bed listening to a recording of Mendelssohn's violin concerto. Ann would not let me speak, and I lay there in the dark, listening to this achingly beautiful music and discovered for the first time that there were composers other than Tchaikovsky, Chopin and Adam. My father was so knowledgeable about music, but the way he rammed it down our throats made it seem like a punishment. Years later I was able to let him know how passionate about music I also became.

One day Ann and I found ourselves outside the Opera Theatre. We noticed that the performance that evening was to be the opera *La Traviata*. Ann said she had heard it was good, and that we should try to see it. Off we went to the box office, where we were firmly told that no tickets were available. Disappointed, we nonetheless decided to walk round the building. We were standing by the stage door when a man came out and saw us. He asked us what we were doing and we explained that we had hoped to go to the performance, but it was sold out. "*Attendez*" he said, and disappeared inside the doorway. He soon reappeared with an envelope, and gave us two tickets for that evening. No charge – free – gratis.

We were so excited, and rushed back to our house to tell the family what we were doing before changing into our 'uniform' of grey pleated skirts, jumpers, blue blazers and 'idler' shoes. When we returned to the Opera the theatre was ablaze with lights, and we gazed with admiration at the beautifully-dressed clientèle. Proudly we presented our tickets, expecting to be shown to the third row on the highest level. To our utter astonishment, we were ushered into the very best seats in the house! These were the 'fauteuils' – armchairs - in the centre of the front row in the dress circle. On either side of us were the most glamorous and sumptuously-dressed opera goers, and they all smiled fondly at us as we scuttled into these fabulous seats. As soon as the opera began I was hooked. Without doubt *La Traviata* holds a very special place in my heart after the experience of hearing this beautiful and ultimately heart-rending opera for the first time in such a perfect setting.

Shortly after this wonderful evening, Ann and I went to the English Church for the Sunday service. The church was packed, and I soon realized why. The guest preacher was Harold Macmillan, who had recently succeeded my uncle as Prime Minister. I felt rather weepy, and reflected that if Uncle A had not been so ill, it would have been him preaching in the church instead. After the service I managed to shake Mr Mac by the hand, and explain who I was. Probably rather embarrassing for him!

Katinka left – and so it was just Ann and I. I became aware that one of the young men in the house was paying me rather a lot of attention. This was Gérard, who was the student at the military academy of St. Cyr. He seemed enormously adult and sophisticated to me, but for some reason he took a liking to me. I had never had a proper boyfriend. I wrote to several boys, but none were serious. Our letters were always a contest to see which one of us could be the funniest. I had had my first kiss when I was fifteen – but that was about it!

One day Gérard suggested I meet him during the day, and he would show me Paris. This first attempt was a disaster, as I was waiting inside the Metro station and he was outside. No mobile telephones in those days. After that we were more explicit about where we would meet.

I fell totally in love with Gérard, and he was extremely kind to me, and did not take advantage of my so obvious innocence.

He called me "Bébé" and I called him "Grandpère", and he offered to teach me what he felt I should know.

It was very romantic. Gérard took me to the Bois de Boulogne, and Versailles, and we walked for miles and miles. All the while he was trying to improve my French even when lying on the grass by Le Petit Trianon. The diminutive concierge, Mlle Collobert, thought we were a lovely young couple, and she would offer us a safe haven in her apartment, where we would take tea and eat delicious little pieces of bread spread with her home-made quince jelly. Gérard and I moved our beds to either side of the curtain, so that we could hold hands under it when we went to sleep!!

It had to end, of course. I came home from my ballet class one day and went up to my room. Suddenly Gérard was there! He had not gone to his school that day. Before I knew it, he had taken me in his arms, and was giving me a passionate embrace. Just then, over his shoulder, who should I see coming up the stairs but Mme. Colombier, our landlady. She roared into the room, and quick as lightning gave us both resounding slaps across our faces! Gérard was banished and I was torn to shreds by a torrent of verbal abuse. We were forbidden to say a single word to each other in the house.

Every morning we had breakfast in the dining room. It was quite delicious – a fresh baguette, French butter and apricot jam, accompanied by hot chocolate. It was the custom for us all to shake hands and say "Bonjour". Gérard and I became quite adept at passing notes to each other and arranging to meet later on. We handled this quite well, and I was careful to be a 'good girl' in the house. Mlle Collobert then became our 'post box' and all messages and billet-doux passed through her hands.

It became time for me to return home for the holidays. I

had informed my parents that I did not want to continue to live with the Colombiers, and please would they find somewhere else. Gérard said he would write to me, and look for somewhere for me as well. I hated saying goodbye to him.

Back in the leafy New Forest, I mooned about dreaming of Gérard. I wrote to him, telling him how much I loved the New Forest, but was also looking forward to returning to Paris – but not to the dreaded Colombiers. I addressed the letter to Mlle. Collobert.

Malheur! Hélas! Désastre! The letter was opened by Mme. Colombier!

Poor Gérard had the most frightful time, and sad to say, I never knew what became of him. He wrote a letter warning me that Mme. C had hit the roof with fury, and was forwarding my letter to my father, and telling him about 'the kiss'. I was sick with fear, as no one could be more fierce than my father when he was angry. True to form, as I entered his room, I could almost see steam coming out of his ears! His eyes flashed, his eyebrows twitched, his moustache bristled, and he positively shook with anger.

"What IS the meaning of all this?" he demanded. Tremulously I tried to explain that while nothing dreadful had happened, Gérard and I had fallen in love. My father was, at heart, a complete romantic. In his way I feel sure he understood what had happened, and forgave me for my girlish passion. What he could NOT forgive, however, was my appalling French, and that I had started the letter by writing "*Ma cher Gérard*"!

I was, *naturellement*, forbidden to contact Gérard again. After a while my heart mended, but I was so disappointed to learn I was not to be allowed to return to Paris. Despite the "*Ma cher Gérard*" my French was improving, and another three months would have done wonders. But no – once again I was on the move.

Ah what was then my misery! Pining with unrequited love for Gérard, and smarting in the atmosphere of disapproval and disgrace, I awaited news of my impending fate.

For once my parents appeared to be in complete agreement, as they huddled together trying to decide what on earth they should do with such a wayward daughter. Eventually it was my mother who told me. She valiantly tried to make it sound exciting as she told me it had been decided that I was to attend a Finishing School in Switzerland. Der Töchterinstitut had come highly recommended and Mummy was SURE I would love it there. The fun thing was I would be enrolled as a "*Haushaltenschülerin*", learning cooking, flower arranging and how to run a house. It wouldn't be like going back to school.

The institute was in a beautiful village called Klosters. The only slight problem was that I would be required to learn German while at the same time perfecting French. I was aghast. It sounded very much like school to me!

It was agreed that Mummy should take me to Klosters herself, and in the preceding weeks she was at her most loving and encouraging. On the 14th May 1957 we boarded the Golden Arrow train and began the journey to Switzerland. I couldn't help becoming a little excited, and Mummy and I had great fun, especially on the French sleeper, which we caught in Calais. I looked out of the train windows in the morning and saw the scenery dramatically changing to wondrous and awe-inspiring mountains. Perhaps this might not be so bad after all, I thought. We took a taxi to the school (which I agree looked pretty in a typical Swiss chalet style) and were ushered into the presence of Herr und Frau Doktor, the Principals.

Herr Doktor was tall, thin and grey, while Frau Doktor was tall, sturdy and grey. Every bit of their clothing was grey, even Frau D's stockings and shoes. They smiled – with their lips only. I did not like them.

Immediately Mummy launched into her flawless German, and soon they were all chatting away and ignoring me. Mummy then explained that I couldn't after all be a *Haushalternschülerin* as there were no vacancies, but it didn't matter as I would only be studying languages, and Italian was added to the list.

I was shown into my room, which I shared with a Dutch girl. It was pretty and had a wonderful view of the Gotschna, the main mountain. Mummy was booked into a lovely small hotel in the village.

I could not believe how homesick I was! I was totally miserable, and cried myself to sleep every night. What had happened to the 'almost-grown-up-girl' from Paris? Every spare minute I rushed down to the village and met Mummy. We went shopping and drank delicious hot chocolate or *Eiskaffee*. I dreaded the day of her departure.

There was one other English-speaking pupil at the school, and she was Australian. She was called Robin Falstein and became a great friend. All the other girls were nice, and the German and Dutch girls all spoke perfect English. The French and the Italian girls were useless at languages, and were as homesick as I was.

When the awful day of Mummy's departure came, my new friends gathered around me and all came to the station with me to see her off. Immediately she had gone they gathered me up and jollied me along and to my surprise, I actually felt much better. I entered into the life of the institute, and promptly became a thorn in the side of the Doktors!

We were up every morning at 6.30 for exercises in the garden, led by Herr Doktor. Exercise was no problem for me as I was used to a daily ballet class – but I still mucked around and behaved badly. After breakfast we had our lessons all morning.

Our main teacher was a woman called Frau Gurzer. I rapidly decided that there was something very odd about Frau Gurzer. Her looks were completely unremarkable in a somewhat messy, 'put together' frame. She was jolly, in a loud, obtrusive way, and endlessly trying to ingratiate herself with the pupils and appear to be 'one of us'. Frau Gurzer could speak a little English, whereas the Doktors spoke none. Frau Doktor made it quite clear that she thought I was only pretending not to understand German, as my mother was so fluent.

All our laundry was collected in the basement and laid out on shelves once clean. I happened to go there one day and found Frau Gurzer going through the shelves and picking out clothes.

"Frau Gurzer!" I said, "What on earth are you doing?" FG jumped like a startled rabbit and fumbled an explanation about trying to sort out a muddle of clothes. Me being me, I believed her, and thought no more about it.

FG was meant to teach us German. She didn't do very well. One day she told us we would all have an English class, and Elfie and Robin would be the teachers and she would be a pupil. "Shakespeare!" she said. "Wonderful man. "To be or not to be – that is the question." In German – "*Sein oder nicht sein – das ist die Frage!*" or "My horse, my horse, my kingdom for my horse!" – in German, "*Mein Pferd, mein Pferd, mein Königreich für ein Pferd!*"

FG then insisted on sitting in my place, and made me take a lesson in English. Suddenly we heard the unmistakable tread of Herr Doktor trying to creep stealthily down the passage to eavesdrop on our class. FG whispered to me to point to the blackboard, and we then chanted in unison the well-known Shakespearian phrases. HD left, deeply satisfied that we were learning so much.

During the afternoons we went on expeditions. They were really quite fun, but Robin and I were so naughty and full of rebellion that we often didn't allow ourselves to enjoy them. Robin, at seventeen and a half, was a year older than I. She was also far more sophisticated, and her life in Sydney had been much freer than even my three liberating months in Paris.

I do remember feeling incredibly sick when we went round the Maggi factory and saw how sweet little calves were turned into tiny cubes of stock! Lectures in art galleries left us completely cold. But we both enjoyed driving round the country and going on long walks.

The height was affecting me, and on several occasions I either very nearly, or actually, fell into a faint. One day up a mountain I had to lie in a darkened room suffering from a chronic headache the like of which I had never had before. Nobody thought to get me to a lower altitude though, and I realise now I was quite lucky not to have been more adversely affected.

Robin was 'into boys'. There were plenty of them in the village. Occasionally we were allowed to bathe in the public swimming pool, and that gave us an opportunity to get to know a few of the local likely lads.

One day Robin and I were lagging behind on a mountain trek. We had travelled to this area by bus, and when we finally reached the place where the bus was parked – it had gone!

We realised we would be in dreadful trouble, and set off to walk back along the road. Suddenly there was the beeping of a horn and a car drew alongside with two of the village boys inside. Naturally they offered to drive us back, and naturally we accepted. Soon we saw the bus ahead of us, but instead of trying to stop it so we could join the others, the boys sped past it laughing and Robin and I tried to hide our heads.

Back in the village we had to thank our friends, so we all had a hot chocolate before R and I slunk back to the school. Well, we were severely punished, which undoubtedly we deserved. On a glorious Saturday, when the whole school was allowed out to go where they liked, Robin and I were incarcerated in separate classrooms, writing lines in Deutsch, supervised by dear Frau Gurzer – she who had not waited the extra five minutes for us and therefore caused most of the trouble.

The time of year was of course summer. Robin and I wanted to sunbathe, discreetly, so off we went, up the mountain, and found a glorious spot, totally private, on the top of a wonderful grassy meadow. When the time came to leave we did what any sensible New Forest or Sydney girl would do – we rolled down the mountain.

Next day we were summoned to the presence of the Grey Ones. Their faces were incredulous. NEVER in the history of the Töchterinstitut had any pupil ever done anything so wicked as to *ROLL DOWN A MOUNTAIN*!

We tried to look suitably contrite. We could not imagine who had seen us, but seen and recognised we had been. So more punishment was meted out.

The boys in the village were not only interested in Robin and me. The other girls all had little flirtations as well, and one night my room-mate Margita and I were awoken by excited whispers informing us that the boys were in our garden.

Robin had a room all to herself, and her windows opened

directly onto the garden just one easy floor up. Soon Robin's room was full of German, French, Italian and Dutch girls, as they communicated with the boys outside. Then, panic, shouts of anger and a barking dog, and Herr Doktor in his night robes came rushing out to chase the boys away. All the girls hid on the floor in Robin's room trying hard to stifle their giggles. When HD went away the boys silently came back, and one or two of them climbed up onto Robin's window sill and flirted outrageously with the German girls!

Mummy never wrote to me – she didn't have time, as she was so busy running the schools. However, from time to time she telephoned me. This was great fun and I was able to assure her I was having a good time, and that Robin and I had become great friends. Mummy was delighted, as she had enjoyed meeting Robin when she had been in Klosters. This was to stand me in very good stead, as I was to discover later.

Frau Gurzer continued to behave in an erratic way, and it wasn't only Robin and I who noticed this. She was endlessly telling tales on us, and then apologising madly. On one occasion she actually made up a misdemeanour. For once Robin and I were totally innocent, but the HDs were so furious that they threatened to expel both of us. No matter how hard we protested our innocence, they refused to believe us. We were gated for an entire weekend, with copious lines to write and learn. We smarted from the injustice. We took our punishments well when they were deserved – but for something we didn't do – that was too much!

A week later (by which time R and I were really hating FG and watching her carefully) we were both sitting at her table during our evening meal. Robin happened to say to me that she had not been sleeping well for the past few nights. The following day was her birthday, and I said, "Oh Robin, you must sleep well tonight so you can enjoy your birthday tomorrow". Frau Gurzer overheard this exchange, and pronounced that she would give Robin something that would ensure she had a good sleep that night.

I was in Robin's room after supper when FG burst in unannounced with a spoon in her hand. "Open your mouth, Robin" she said, and as Robin looked aghast at the spoon and cried "SIX!" – FG shoved the pills down her throat. It all happened so quickly, but I said, "Frau Gurzer – why did you give her six tablets?" and luckily this was overheard by an English-speaking German girl.

"It's OK, OK" she assured us. "You sleep well, Robin".

The following morning I awoke and quickly ran down to Robin's room. She was completely and utterly asleep. I could not stir her at all. As it was her birthday, I decided not to continue to try and awaken her, but to let her sleep on. I locked Robin's door and pocketed the key, then kept it on me while I did my morning exercises.

When I went upstairs again there was pandemonium outside Robin's room. Frau Gurzer was hammering on her door and shouting for her at the top of her voice. Several of the other girls hovered near by looking puzzled.

I immediately said, "Stop hammering on the door – I have the key." In a frenzied movement FG snatched it from me and burst into Robin's room. Shouting her name all the while, FG shook Robin roughly, but there was no response. Suddenly I began to be afraid. "What have you done, Frau Gurzer?" I demanded. "What did you give her last night?"

FG did not answer, but instead picked up the jug of water which we used every morning for washing and threw the entire contents over Robin's face. There was still no reaction from her.

When the bell rang, Frau Gurzer tried to make me go to my lessons. I refused, as by now I realised that it was the pills she had given Robin which were causing her to be in this dire situation. I stood my ground and totally refused to leave Robin.

Everyone else left. I shut the door and did my best to make the bed dry with some towels, and all the while I gently tried to wake her up. Naïve, stupid and innocent as was, I knew I just had to get her to wake up. At last she moaned, and made a valiant effort to open her eyes.

A good hour later the door burst open and in strode Frau Doktor. She had given up speaking to me in German by now and we spoke in French. FD ordered me to go to my classes. I refused, and in turn ordered her to get a doctor. She advanced towards me, six feet of grey-clad dourness, and struck me resoundingly on my face. First in Paris and now in Switzerland!

Well – that did it. My blood was up and the temper that my mother was always telling me I had inherited from my father came to the fore. There was no way I was going to leave Robin until she woke up. FD conceded and left me to it.

For the entire day no member of staff came anywhere near us. A friendly German girl managed to smuggle some bread out of the dining room for me to keep hunger at bay.

At about 6.30pm a fellow pupil knocked on the door and told me I was wanted on the telephone. I asked her to stay with Robin while I went to answer it.

"Hello" I said, and the international operator said, "Are you Robin?" and I said "No, I am Elfrida." "Oh" said the operator, "We have just been told you were too ill to talk." "No," said I, "I am fine. It is Robin who is too ill."

Then, so incredibly fortunately, I found myself speaking to my darling mama. I told her everything and she was furious, and somewhat panicking about Robin as well.

"Put Frau Doktor on the telephone at once!" she said. I opened the door of the study and FD practically fell into the room, as she had been desperately trying to understand what I had been saying.

My mother let her have it. "You get a doctor to that child this instant or take her directly to the hospital, and in the meantime I am informing her father about the shocking way you have been neglecting her!" she thundered.

I returned to Robin's room, where she was still deeply comatose. About an hour later the door was flung open and the Fraus D and G pushed me unceremoniously out of the room in order to let the doctor in. I retired to my own room – exhausted.

Robin recovered, thankfully, but not for a day or two. This episode cemented our friendship, but with my older and wiser head I now don't think I did enough. I was completely unaware of the dangers of overdosing on sleeping tablets, especially at a high altitude. It was so incredibly fortunate that Mummy chose to ring me that night, and that when she heard I was too ill to talk she had immediately asked for Robin. Without her intervention, goodness knows what might have happened.

Once back in England I was summoned to Heathrow to collect a large parcel. It contained a huge koala bear which Robin's father had sent me as a thank you present. I loved that koala for years.

The final drama happened just before the end of term. Frau Gurzer had been in disgrace after the sleeping tablet episode and for some reason, HD decided to enter her room one day when she was out. There she discovered item after item of supposedly 'lost' articles of clothing belonging to the pupils. Wrapped up and ready to go were two parcels, addressed to FG in Germany. It then transpired that we weren't the only ones having problems with FG, and that she had systematically lied and stolen goods from her previous job as well.

I have to admit that it was rather satisfying seeing Herr and Frau Doktor having to eat humble pie and apologise to, of all people, Robin and me for the wrongs done to us! They realised that the FG had indeed made trouble for us. Although we knew we had deserved some punishment, it was not quite as much as was meted out to us. We were awfully gracious and accepted their apologies kindly.

By this time my parents – wait for it – had decided I should not return to Switzerland. After all I had gone through, I was disappointed. My German was coming along (although my Italian, taught in German, was less good) and everyone said the best term was during the winter, when we all learned to ski.

No – they were adamant I should leave. Before I left, I gave a performance. My ambition had always been to dance *The Dying Swan*. This was the music by Saint-Saens that the Hungarian musicians had played the minute I walked in to have tea in Claridges Hotel with my mother when I was a little girl.

The room was cleared, and somehow, with the help of my international friends, I created a swan-like costume and danced this solo to the very best of my ability. I wrote in my diary, "I really felt I had truly died". Even Frau Doktor smiled – with her eyes! The sting of her slap on my face had receded, but I wondered if it would happen to me again at the next place I would be visiting.

I cried bitterly at leaving Klosters and treasure my book of photos and messages from all my friends. It was especially hard saying goodbye to Robin, but we had a plan to meet up in England in the future. When Robin did come and stay with us later on she told me the winter term had been sensational. They had hardly done any lessons, and they all learned to ski brilliantly, plus somehow the German language just fell into place. I certainly missed out on that one.

★ ★ ★

After leaving Switzerland, I spent most of the summer holidays at Fritham. Robin came and stayed, which was huge fun, and everybody liked her. Our extended family also included not only Veronica but dear Marianne von Wimpffen. Marianne originally applied for a job in the school, but being Austrian and lovely, she rapidly became another honorary member of our family, and not only lived with us for years but appeared in the formal photographs of us girls and our mother. Marianne often looked after me when I was living almost alone in London. She was a wonderful cook and became a dear friend to us all.

Back in London with Robin, Mia and Marianne, life continued its usual pattern; ballet classes, church every Sunday, going to the cinema whenever we could and always dreaming about boys. I was therefore rather taken aback when my mother called me into her room one day in order to introduce me to a little girl called Patricia. Mummy explained that Patricia's father was a diplomat based in Germany and they were looking for someone to be a companion and part-time tutor to her.

I thought this little girl was sweet. I liked all children, and as I had so often helped out in the school and taught a wide variety of classes I felt I was more than qualified to accept. I would also have the opportunity to continue my studies in German. I was glad I was not to be sent to another scholastic establishment. As I was now 17 years old, I felt completely grown up.

The Ms were a charming family. They treated me as an adult

and welcomed me into their home in Bad Godesberg. I had a
very nice room, and I enjoyed being with Patricia.

The little girl attended the French Lycée, where I delivered
and collected her every day. There was a charming couple in the
house, both Italian, who cooked and did the housework. I was
able to practise my limited Italian on them. On normal days I
ate with the family in the evenings, unless they were
entertaining. It was all extremely civilised.

Patricia made some friends at school, and in our area there
were several English children, so I soon I found myself giving
ballet classes in the basement. I also gave Patricia lessons in
English and maths. This was about the only standard of maths I
could cope with!

Twice a week a young man called Robert came to the house
to give me German lessons. Robert was small, neat, pedantic and
serious. He had a round face and wore round glasses. He wore
an overcoat, carried a furled umbrella and wore a hat. Not my
type at all. Not a Gérard or a Klosters boy! His lessons were
rather dull, but I suppose something stuck along the way.

Life was fairly uneventful, and my only complaint was that
I never had any proper time off. Then I met another English girl
working for an American family. Antonia was in charge of the
seven-year-old and there was another nanny for the baby.
Antonia never had a single moment free, and whenever she had
some spare time, she had to remove the little balls of fluff from
the children's woolly clothes.

On two memorable occasions Robert was allowed to take
me 'out on the town' at night. During the first one he took me
to see a film. It was an English film, but dubbed into German
and impossible to understand. On the second outing I managed
to persuade Robert to take us to a club. Shock, horror – how

decadent! The name escapes me now – the Cave? The Den? It matters not. It was fun and buzzing and the first bit of 'life' I had seen since arriving in Germany.

There was a live band, and they were inviting members of the audience to come up and sing. To Robert's mortification, I volunteered. The only problem was that the band did not know the song I wanted to sing and felt I could do quite well. Instead they persuaded me to sing the Johnny Ray song "I never felt more like singing the blues…" which I really did not know. I think I was perfectly dreadful, but nobody seemed to care, and the whole evening was huge fun.

The Ms went away for a week and I was in charge. Every night I sat in the dining room and the Italian butler served my meal. He also poured me a nice glass of red wine, which I thoroughly enjoyed. It wasn't until the Ms returned that I found out I had been casually drinking his best vintage port! I still have a good taste for port, but try not to drink it in wine glasses.

Jussi Björling, the famous Swedish tenor, died while I was in Bad Godesberg. I had been lucky enough to have heard him in person at the Royal Albert Hall the year before. I will never forget him standing perfectly still on the stage before a packed house until every last cough, splutter, sneeze or rustle had been silenced. Only then did he begin to sing, and it was at that moment I understood the word 'sublime'. It was a magical and beautiful evening.

The radio in Germany played a tribute to Jussi, and I lay in the dark listening to his fabulous voice and thinking that nothing could be more perfect.

The time was approaching when I would be launched into society as a debutante.

My mother had already started on the rounds of Ladies'

Luncheons. Most of my contemporaries were finishing their studies at Mme. Katinka's in Paris. Only I had had such an odd year, and finished it with a smattering of German and Italian and slightly more French, but no proper qualification anywhere.

Before returning to England I decided to have my hair done in Bonn. I looked up 'trim' in the dictionary, but must have got it wrong! My usual rather boring head of hair was almost shorn, as I was given the then quite fashionable 'urchin cut'. I knew my mother would freak, but I rather liked it. My early debutante photos show this new hair style.

I didn't cry on leaving Germany, but I was grateful to the Ms for having given me such a nice time. Lady M. was to involve me in a rather bizarre situation the following year. More of that later.

CHAPTER TEN

COMING OUT

I had always known that one day I would be a debutante, but I had no idea our year would turn out to be so significant. 1958 was the last year debutantes were presented at Court to Her Majesty the Queen. I consider myself fortunate to have been the right age at the right time.

The popular conception about debutantes now is that they are a lot of silly, spoilt, rich young girls who wear white ball gowns and curtsey to cakes. This is an inaccurate and muddled description of a tradition that went back well over a hundred years. The London Season, when debutantes were introduced into society, runs from April to July. As neither hunting nor shooting can take place during these months, the main social activities take place in and around the capital. In the 1800s and 1900s, entire households would decamp from their country estates to reside in London for the festivities. Young girls of the right age, who up to that time would most likely have spent their whole life in the country being educated in reading, music, dance, needlework and not much more, would be brought to London in order to find a husband.

Before being launched into society at large, the young ladies were presented to Their Majesties. It was then very important for these young girls to be seen at all the important occasions, whether they were gallery openings, horse races, theatrical events or even card parties, to prove how worthy they would be as grand hostesses.

Mothers were desperate to find suitably grand husbands for their daughters, while the young gentlemen would be on the hunt for attractive maidens with not only good genes and common sense, but hopefully an enticing dowry as well!

The Season continued in this manner unabated until the 20th century. Gradually the young girls became more educated and travelled abroad to perfect languages and broaden their horizons, but the main objective was still pretty much the same. The wars rather naturally caused a certain amount of disruption and during World War Two many future debutantes found themselves working in munitions factories, driving ambulances or becoming auxiliary nurses, which succeeded in changing their outlook on the Season. Court presentations had been suspended for the duration of the war, and when they were reintroduced there was such a backlog of girls that the King and Queen decided to forego the formal evening presentations and give large afternoon garden parties instead. A debutante could consider herself launched into society if she managed to drop a curtsey to the King or Queen, even if they were in the distance.

Teatime presentations were then adopted, and initially these were held on one day only. A girl could only be presented by someone who had been presented herself. Usually this would be the girl's mother, but often a grandmother, godmother or aunt would fill this role. By the time I came along, the one day had stretched to three and many girls were introduced by ladies who for a fee had agreed to bring two or three girls out into society as their protégées. Queen Elizabeth II decided that enough was enough, and decreed that the Court Presentations would cease. This was right, in my opinion, although I would have been chagrined if they had ended in 1957.

Queen Charlotte's Ball became the focus of the season. This dance raises money for the Queen Charlotte's hospital, which is named after the wife of George III. Having no children of her own, Queen Charlotte had her ladies in waiting present her each year with a large birthday cake, and after her death it became the tradition to commemorate her birthday with a ball designed to raise money for her hospital. The debutantes represent the ladies in waiting, and they curtsy not to the cake but to the guest of honour, who in turn represents Queen Charlotte herself.

Even in the 1950s it was still not considered terribly important for girls to be brilliantly educated. Most girls had been abroad to perfect a language or study history of art or music. Many of my friends were also doing secretarial courses or going to finishing schools, as I was supposed to have done in Switzerland. Social manners, flower arranging and simple cookery were all considered important. With my weird education and concentration on dancing, and with no knowledge whatsoever of countryside pursuits, I would never have passed the rigorous tests set out for the young girls in the Regency period. In no way was I suitable wife material!

In 1958 there were many girls who became debutantes just to be presented at court. These girls then retreated back to their country lives with, no doubt, sighs of relief. My friends and I were different. We were determined to enjoy every minute of it.

While I had been living in Germany, my mother had been attending Mother's Lunch parties. She thoroughly enjoyed these, and made some good new friends. Soon after the Christmas holiday season was over I started going to girls' tea parties. At these parties we met up with old friends, made some new ones and exchanged addresses. My mother arranged for me to give my two parties at the Ritz hotel. Photographs show us all dressed exactly like our mothers and pretending to be seriously grown up.

After the tea parties came the cocktail parties, and it was at these that we began to meet the young men who hoped they would all become Debs' Delights. Girls with older brothers had a huge advantage, whereas people like me had hardly met any boys their own age. I fell in and out love with increasing rapidity as the Season wore on. After a few drinks, when I began to relax somewhat, I could be persuaded to show my dancing and provided I was wearing suitable clothes, to kick my leg over brave boys standing in front of me!

Although I had accepted I would not be a ballerina, I still went to class every day. I was also constantly asked to perform at small events and appeared occasionally on TV.

March 20th was the date of my presentation, and Alexandra Versen (Colquhoun) and I went with our mothers in a hired limousine. We lined up in the Mall, and crowds of onlookers were waving, cheering and wishing us luck. Some young men in an open-topped car drove around the statue of Queen Victoria with a placard saying "GOODBYE DEAR DEBS!"

Photographers were everywhere, and I was also being photographed by a wonderful woman called Inge Morath, who was taking the pictures for articles in French and German magazines. Miss Morath later married the American playwright Arthur Miller, after he had divorced Marilyn Monroe.

The Queen and the Duke of Edinburgh must have been counting the hours and minutes as they at last saw a light at the end of the tunnel. For us, though, it was a huge treat, to hear one's name called and to walk the length of the throne room before sinking into the deep court curtsey before each of them. Thankfully we were in short dresses. How hard it would have been in the olden days with not just long dresses but trains as well to contend with.

The tea afterwards was delicious and the chocolate cake lived up to its reputation. I dawdled on the grand staircase, slowly descending step by step and savouring every moment. I was the last to leave the palace, although not the last to be presented.

The Season then started in earnest, with more cocktail parties followed now by dances. My mother had managed to go to New York while I was abroad, and she had returned with masses of wonderful clothes, which amazingly I really liked. For once she hadn't gone mad with frills, and some of them were so good we had them copied in different colours. Everything seemed to fit, including the beautiful dress for my own dance. Fifty years later this dress was among several other lovely dresses that were featured in an exhibition held at Kensington Palace. I stood behind my dress and was somewhat put out to note that I could no longer fit into the 22" waist!

That exhibition at Kensington Palace was an opportunity to meet up with the 1958 debutantes and discover the directions their lives had taken. Fiona MacCarthy had been admired by the rest of us, as she was so brainy. A serious 'bluestocking' with a university degree, Fiona became a successful journalist and author.

To commemorate the fiftieth anniversary of our debutante season, Fiona and I appeared in several radio and television shows together. Fiona had also written a book about our year called *THE LAST CURTSEY*. We discovered that most of us were married with grandchildren, but I think I was alone in running a dancing school. Some became successful in the media world, while others became renowned painters and authors. Several girls made 'good' marriages, and a surprising amount had become magistrates, school governors or presidents of charities. The list goes on, and friendships were renewed. There were many stories of successes and sadly, some tragedies. The exhibition brought back so many memories of a few months in our lives just being "giddy young girls". I even managed to demonstrate the court curtsey on film, despite a dodgy knee.

My dance was held at home. Home was also, of course, the school. After the children had left, all the school furniture and paraphernalia were packed up and stored overnight. Every door was removed, and my lovely teacher Enid and her talented husband Gordon created a scene in yellow by using yards of netting and quirky string bags full of oranges and lemons. The effect was magical and so clever.

The two well-known bands were Tommy Kinsman and Chappie d'Amato. Despite the fact that I had kissed Tommy Kinsman's drummer when I was 13 as part of a game, and had then been allowed to sign his drum, Mummy had chosen Chappie d'Amato, as he had played for my sisters as well. Our wonderful room with its vaulted ceiling came into its own. We also gave a dinner party in a beautifully-transformed classroom earlier, and to my joy my father was present, looking so elegant in white tie. The photograph taken by Barry Swaebe before the dance is the only one I have of me with my parents.

I loved my dance, and thought my mother was so clever to have given it early in the season. My string bags looked fun then, but compared with a whole ballroom decorated with a desert theme, complete with sand, oasis and a live camel, or another dance where a replica of Brighton Pavilion was silhouetted against a starlit night sky, they looked distinctly amateur!

Country dances were my favourite. Inevitably these ended in the small hours of the morning, and couples could be seen entwined and shrouded in the early mists of a summer's day stealing kisses under the trees. Breakfast at 2 am was a must. This was usually kedgeree, and then we'd return to the hosts who had kindly put us up for the night and sleep most of the next day!

We were beastly about the boys, and gave them labels such as NSIT (not safe in taxis), MTF (must touch flesh) or even MSC (makes skin creep). I am sure however that they were equally cruel about us. Good-looking, well-mannered boys, especially if they had cars, were hugely in demand. Good manners were very important. Young men had to dance with every girl in their dinner party, and everybody was expected to write polite thank-you letters as soon as possible.

The Berkeley Dress Show was an important event, and I felt sure that with my slender figure and dancer's posture I would be picked. Unfortunately for me Pierre Cardin was chosen to show his clothes that year, and they were all far too small for me.

I decided it would be fun to smoke. After my trial in Paris with Gauloises, I had forgotten about smoking for a while, but now as a deb it seemed quite the thing.

First of all I smoked cocktail cigarettes. They were so pretty in pink, mauve, green and gold. Then I went for sophistication, with Black Sobranis. To make these dark cigarettes even more exciting, I began to collect long cigarette holders. The best one I had would extend to three times its length by the end of the evening. It required all my sucking power to get the cigarette at the end to glow! To complete my smoking ensemble I carried a dear little portable ashtray with a flower-decorated lid. Yes – it was definitely fun to smoke!

A few years later I found I had bought a pack of proper cigarettes just for myself. I instantly decided to give up, although we still provided cigarettes for guests in various silver boxes and especially for the relaxing smoke in between courses at a dinner party.

We were supposedly the 'last-ever debs' and as a result we received a ridiculous amount of publicity. Because of my well-known family name I was constantly photographed and quoted, often in the most banal way. I once commented that some chap had trodden on my toe and that this had given me a blister. This prompted an outraged letter in one of the daily newspapers castigating the young men for not learning how to dance properly! We were hardly out of the news, and began to feel we were indeed rather famous. I appeared on TV with Barbara Cartland when she was the subject of *This Is Your Life*, and was asked to give talks to women's groups. My photo taken by Betty Swaebe in my swan costume was the front piece of a glossy magazine, and this resulted in an offer to dance on TV as well as surprising a few of my fellow debs and their delights.

We attended film premieres, including the film of *The Reluctant Debutante,* which previously had been a stage show starring our friend Anna Massey. We met up for picnics at Royal Ascot, Henley and Wimbledon, and it would be fair to say that for these few months we lived the life of Riley. We were indeed spoilt and pampered, but we were also learning to grow up and behave in polite society. The Season also gave trade to thousands of caterers, florists, photographers, marquee and taxi companies and so forth, all of whom must have deeply regretted the demise of the debutantes.

It did continue after a fashion for several years, albeit with no presentations, and I was called upon to teach latter-day debs to perform the court curtsey correctly when the Queen Charlotte's Ball was reinstated. This proved quite hard on occasion, as the modern young girls insisted on wearing Doc Marten boots!

I did not continue the season in Ireland and Scotland as many of my peers did in 1958. I rather wish I had, but at the time I was 'partied out' and quite anxious to get on with my career, which was definitely veering towards a life in the theatre.

★ ★ ★

During my year as a debutante I was lucky enough to have been invited to a few film premieres. One of these, cleverly timed, was *The Reluctant Debutante*. The actress Diane Clare, who starred in the film, later became a good friend of mine when we met again dog walking in the park.

I used to love dressing up for premieres, and on one occasion I was photographed with the star of the film at the Odeon Leicester Square. It was therefore with great excitement that I accepted the invitation from my former employer in Germany, Lady M, to join her for tea at the Dorchester Hotel, where she said she would introduce me to an American actress who was starring in a film about to be premiered in London.

I tried to hide my disappointment when I met the actress. For a start she wore no make-up, and to my eyes she looked distinctly plain. Her clothes were dull, and altogether I thought no one could have looked less like a film star.

We chatted, and I was asked all sorts of questions about my life and my family. At the end of tea the actress formally invited me to attend the premiere of her film the following week as her guest, and to attend a dinner afterwards in the last remaining privately owned house in Berkeley Square.

I chose my outfit for this occasion very carefully. I had recently bought a stunning (or so I thought) outfit in a leopard print. Tight trousers were worn underneath a fairly figure-hugging tunic. I admit I thought I looked the 'bees knees' – or at least the 'leopard's spots'!

It was important, I decided, to make a good impression when I arrived, as there were bound to be ranks of photographers outside the cinema. I decided to be my mother's daughter, and hired a limousine from Queensbury Hire with uniformed chauffeur.

Warning bells began to ring when the car drove me not to the West End, but to an obscure cinema in Victoria. I swept up in all my finery, but where were the crowds and the photographers? Nary a one to be seen. I dismissed the car, as I had been assured someone would take me to dinner and see me home.

Inside the cinema, I suddenly realised that I had made a complete fool of myself. I was the only person dressed to kill. Everyone else wore sensible day clothes, and none of the women wore any make-up or jewels.

I was immediately put in the charge of an extremely friendly girl called Sarah. As I sat next to her in the auditorium, she whispered to me that her father was going to say a few words before the film. I had not the faintest idea what he was talking about, but the same words were repeated several times: 'Moral Rearmament'.

The film was boring and my 'film star' friend was as dull on the screen as off it. If I had been wiser, I would have cut and run, but Sarah never let me out of her sight.

The house in Berkeley Square was impressively huge. The reception was on the first floor up a wide marble staircase. As we walked in I saw waiters carrying trays of drinks, and I thought to myself, "Thank goodness. What I need now is a shot of sustaining alcohol to calm my nerves." Sadly for me, the alcohol turned out to be apple juice.

Sarah told me I had to meet someone very important. I was introduced to a man in a wheelchair and told he was the founder of Moral Rearmament and his name was Dr Frank Buchman. He was a very old man, and he told me he knew all about me. He was acquainted with my uncle and brother (at that time a Member of Parliament) and he knew of my ambitions to dance and act as a profession. He tried to make me promise, then and there, that I would give up all such ideas, and that from that moment on I would devote myself to the family of MRA, excluding all other family members from my life.

To say I was stunned would have been putting it mildly. This whole evening was turning into a nightmare. We were ushered into dinner, and I found myself sitting next to an MP who also knew my brother.

"Oh my goodness" I said, "What on earth is going on? I am totally confused."

"Don't be" he said, "You have been invited to join the wonderful family of MRA and this is your opportunity to really make a difference in the world and devote your life to other people."

"Heavens!" I thought, "he is one of them." (He truly was – he eventually married Sarah). I decided I had to escape. I pretended I had to go to the ladies' room, and feeling quite terrified, I dashed down the huge staircase to the front door – which I couldn't open! Mercifully there was a doorman, and he opened it for me, and I rushed into the bustle of night time Berkeley Square, and amazingly found a taxi.

Sarah didn't give up on me. I was pestered for months to come. Telephone calls, letters, invitations, requests to go to their HQ in Switzerland, and so on. Eventually my dear brother came to the rescue, and spoke firmly to his fellow MP and insisted I must be left alone.

Another lesson in life – and another step up the rung of the ladder called growing up.

CHAPTER ELEVEN

FLIRTING WITH THE STAGE

When I was fifteen, my mother had lent our large room to a group of young socialites who were presenting a play called *The Lights Were Amber* for charity. The condition my mother imposed was that I should have a part in it. Somewhat incongruously, the author, Charles MacArthur Hardy, inserted a can-can dance number to take place in the drawing room of this drawing room farce. I was the lead dancer, but curiously I was not to wear a gorgeous can-can skirt but instead appear in the tutu and danced *sur les pointes*.

My dancing partner was the only professional in the cast, and he was a beast. Quite rightly he thought the whole venture was absurd, and he took it out on me. He rehearsed me until I was exhausted, and pinched me so hard that my body was a mass of bruises. Other than that it was an amusing experience, and I was very proud to be able to say in later years that the soon-to-be very famous actress Susan Hampshire was in the chorus. Years later we would laugh about this experience.

The play was taken to Chatham's naval base before London, and during a reception held for us I met the most divine young man, who looked simply splendid in his navy blue uniform with red stripes down the sides of his trousers. I begged him to come and see the show on the last night and he promised he would. I bought him two tickets right in the centre of the stalls. Full of excitement, I danced my very best with my horrible partner, and as I finished in a flourish by doing the splits, two empty seats in the stalls glared out at me and I suffered the first of many crushing hurts in the pursuit of romance.

Three years later my mother once again allowed a young man to use our hall in which to make his first film. Once again the deal was that I should have a part, so that is how I came to have an extremely small non-speaking part in the first film made by Michael Winner!

The Season was over for the time being, and I began to think seriously about what lay ahead. Mummy had other ideas though. When the lovely Inge Morath was photographing me, I had a session with dress designer Norman Hartnell, and was even made to look like one of his models. Of course –I could be a mannequin! No problem. I had the figure, I had the grace. As far as Mummy was concerned, it was a 'no brainer'.

Once again Mummy had strings to pull. She had become friendly with a delightful French woman called Mme Ginette Spanier, who was head of the House of Balmain. I was to present myself to her the following week in Paris. It did not occur to my mother or me to maybe ask some advice about modelling clothes before I left. My ballet training would surely be enough.

I had not returned to Paris since my student days, and as this was to be a 'flying visit', literally, Mama booked me into the immensely grand Hotel Meurice as well as buying me a ticket on a BEA flight. This was to be my first flight (apart from the escape from Lisbon), and I was tremendously excited.

Seated behind me on the aeroplane was a small boy, also on his first flight. "When are we going to blast off, Daddy?" he enquired, and suddenly I had visions of us hurtling through the skies above accompanied by 'after burners'. I wasn't far wrong!

I was met by a Thomas Cook representative who drove me at once to the House of Balmain. Everyone was very courteous as I walked as normal, but despite my good figure and my ballet training it was not enough. Somewhat surprisingly, I went to see the Colombier family and they graciously gave me a drink before I was engulfed in the splendours of the Hotel Meurice. The next day saw me 'blasting' back to London, and all thoughts of modelling were left behind in Paris.

Mummy wasn't going to give up on me just yet. One day she rushed into my bedroom, threw an envelope down on the bed and said, "There, you said you wanted to act, so I've got you an audition at RADA."

I had never in my wildest dreams considered applying for a place at RADA, the top dramatic school in the country, but I was incapable of saying I did not want to do it. I had one week to learn Juliet's speech, when she takes the sleeping draught the monk gives her. This time two friends were bullied into helping me. One had been a BBC announcer (only correct English in those days), while the other appeared regularly as an actor in the

Whitehall farces. Their advice was somewhat contradictory, and consequently I was woefully underprepared by the time I found myself standing in the wings of the theatre at RADA. I was almost sick with nerves, made worse by the extremely confident, and to my ears brilliant, performance of the girl ahead of me. She virtually skipped off the stage, flashing me a happy smile as she said, "How was I?"

"Wonderful," I muttered before I ventured onto the stage.

"Start!" called a disembodied voice from the auditorium.

"Come vial…" came a satisfyingly tremulous voice from me.

"Thank you, we'll let you know" the disembodied voice cut in. That signalled the end of my hopes of getting into RADA.

The following month I found myself a drama teacher, and began some much-needed classes to improve my technique. I also told Mummy I wanted to have some singing lessons, to see if I could sing.

Two little children attended Lady Eden's School at that time, and their surname was Luft. They were in fact the children of Judy Garland and Sid Luft, and they were living in London for several months.

"You are to go and sing for Judy Garland" my mother announced, "and she will say whether or not you would benefit from lessons."

Oh no, not again! I was in total panic. Sing for Judy Garland? She was just about the most famous singer in the world at that time. What should I sing? I could play a few songs on the piano, so I chose a very old song called "Lover Come Back to Me".

Judy Garland had rented a wonderful old house in Chelsea. I nervously walked up the path and was amazed when Miss Garland herself opened the front door. She showed me into a vast reception room which contained a grand piano. Judy was dressed in black leggings and an oversized red shirt. She made no attempt to talk to me or ask me anything about myself. It was apparent that she was bored rigid at the thought of having to hear me at all.

"Sing!" she commanded. I then discovered I had to accompany myself, and this was NOT a good idea. I tremulously did my best (which was awful). "Continue with your lessons" said Miss Garland, and she left the room. I crept out of the grand house, my cheeks aflame with shame and embarrassment. To this day, whenever I pass that house I relive those awful moments. However, at least I can say I met the famous and extraordinarily talented Judy Garland, even if I would rather forget the circumstances.

It was therefore with huge trepidation that I attended my first singing lesson in Swiss Cottage with a most wonderful, enchanting, diminutive singer called Gwen Catley who in her heyday was famous for having the "highest coloratura voice in the land". Practically standing on tiptoe (she was only 4'11"), Miss Catley corrected my stance and taught me how to pitch my voice. The sounds that came out of my throat amazed me. Was that really me? Under her tuition I was able to sing, quite commendably, numerous songs from the shows of Ivor Novello, Noel Coward etc. In my best song, 'Vilia', I was even able to reach top C. Miss Catley gave me confidence, but sadly I lacked it elsewhere and never really believed I could sing.

* * *

I was now learning to live with the disappointment of not being able to fulfill my ambition of becoming a classical ballet dancer. On my own initiative I was branching out and learning new

Early photo of my father's family. He is holding the racquet.
Marjorie behind Nicholas and Jack behind Anthony.

My mother, aged four

My parents' wedding day, with Uncle Anthony

The Eden family home, Windlestone Hall, Co. Durham

Only John smiled in this photo taken in Canada!

Wrapped up well with my mother during the Canadian winter, 1942

In Canada. Rose standing on left. Ann 3rd left back row.
Amelia kneeling left and me in the centre.

My first solo, aged five

With Madame Vera Volkova

Lady Eden's School's performance of *Belinda and the Baron*. EE on left and
Alfreda Thorogood as the little slave boy.

Belinda and the Baron - Lucy Fisher, Veronica Waggett and EE

When I won 1st prize for the boys' costume! Anna Massey centre back.

EE aged 14, dancing
with Gonchi

Rehearsing for the National Display of Dancing, 1954

'Prayer', aged 14

10, Downing Street,
Whitehall,

April 26, 1955.

Dear Elfrida

How nice of you to write and congratulate me.
It was very thoughtful of you to wait until the
flood of letters had passed before writing.   It
was a good thing you did, otherwise you might have
got a letter beginning "Dear Madam, I write on behalf
of the Prime Minister to thank you for your letter
of ..."!

I was very pleased to get your letter and to
hear all your news.   Your new dining-room must be
very nice but I hope that they did not let you loose
with the paint-brush during the re-decoration.

*Yours affectionate
uncle
Anthony*

Miss Elfrida Eden.

Letter from Uncle Anthony, 1955, when I had congratulated
him on becoming Prime Minister

Liberace's giant signature, a souvenir of an amusing visit

Off to New York. aged 15, with my mother

With my parents at my
debutante dance, 1958
(photos by Barry Swaebe)

Waiting to go to
the Palace

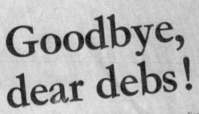

Goodbye, dear debs!

Elfrieda Eden war eine der letzten Debütantinnen am englischen Hof

Featured in a German
magazine, 1958
(photos by Inge Morath)

In my Swan costume aged 17 - photo by Betty Swaebe

With Terry Thomas
at the premiere of
The Reluctant Debutante

Dancing with
Norman Wisdom

HOW I SAID 'NO' TO THREE EAGER SIGNORS

★ *Elfrida Eden, 18-year-old niece of Sir Anthony and sister of Amelia, who married an Italian mechanic in Ischia last September, was reported yesterday to be intending to wed an Italian fisherman in Ischia. Here is her story:*

By ELFRIDA EDEN

IF I'm going to cause a sensation, it will have to be with a prince.

It would be terribly unoriginal to do the same thing as Amelia. But I don't want a life. That's why I'm telling you this—to stop any further speculation right away.

I had three proposals in the fortnight I was in Italy for Amelia's wedding —the first time I had been there.

I loved the cousin—the one who was most handsome. But I would not like to live there.

Romance in Italy is not for me. One month in the family is quite sufficient, thank you.

All the Latin lads did was to scare me with fantastic proposals quite out of the blue.

There I was swimming in about 50 feet of water and trying to cling to a rowing-boat, because I was tired,

when up pops a grinning young Signor.

"Without even saying 'how-do-you-do'," he asks: "Will you become engaged to me?"

I swallowed a mouthful of the Mediterranean, spluttered "No thanks" and dived to the bottom.

This second proposal came a few days before Amelia's wedding at San Angelo Church in Ischia.

This time I had been sunbathing on the beach and was getting ready to go to the hotel.

Another bronzed character stepped in front of me and said "Signorina, will you please become married with me?"

'YOUR BEAUTY'

"Non comprendo," I said. "Goodbye." That was the end of another romance.

Then a letter arrived at my hotel. It said: "I have watched you from afar. Your beauty amazes me. Your hand and heart must be mine in marriage. Forgive me, please."

The letter was post-marked Florence.

There is no romantic Roman in my life. Even in England, I'm completely heart-free.

I am quite happy helping my mother with the telephone she runs and following my ambition to take up a stage career.

Elfrida Eden, away from the Latins, dances with comedian Norman Wisdom.

Lester Piggott cable riddle

Daily Sketch Reporter

JOCKEY Lester Piggott, who was said to have left South Africa after getting a cable that his father was ill, arrived in Nice, on the French Riviera, last night.

Lester under contract till January 17.

Mr. Eades said the cable he referred to in a letter from Lester Piggott.

But, in Nice last night, Lester said: "My contract in South Africa were

Norman Wisdom

Palace Theatre,

LONDON, W.1.

5 February 1959

Dear Elfie,

Thank you for your letter dated 3 February.

It was so nice of you to write and ask me to take out the children of Dr. Barnardo's and to open their fete on May 31st, but I regret that I shall be away at this time, therefore it would be an impossibility. However I am sure that the Fete will be a great success.

I am so glad to hear about your television play and I certainly wish you the best of luck.

Incidentally, I distinctly remember you and I have most certainly not forgotten what I said with regard to having you in the television show and anything that I might consider suitable. The thought is still there.

If you would care to call and see me at the Theatre some evening after the show, which finishes its run on February 21st, I would be delighted. Should you decide to do so my telephone number is REGENT 4101 (Dressing Room) you can phone me any evening.

Yours sincerely,

Norman

Miss Elfrida Eden,
41 Victoria Road,
LONDON, W.8

Letter from Norman Wisdom - I did get an offer from him,
but was forced to refuse it.

EE photographed
by Walter Bird

ELFRIDA HAS 2 PROPOSALS

Amelia and Giovanni with (left) Mrs. Borrelli and Lady (Patricia) Eden, and (right) Mr. Borrelli.

MIRROR CORRESPONDENT
Ischia, Italy, Friday

ELFRIDA EDEN, 18, whose sister Amelia is to marry an Italian ferryboat mechanic here on Sunday, has herself received TWO proposals of marriage from Italians who want aristocratic English brides.

"It's very flattering," Elfrida said today, "but I didn't take them seriously, of course.

"One man wrote to me after seeing my picture in an Italian paper. The other proposed in person.

—But she says NO

"But apart from the fact that I've never met an Italian who comes within six inches of my height (Elfrida is 6ft. tall), I have no wish to get married. I want to go on the stage."

On Holiday

Amelia, 25, a niece of Sir Anthony Eden, met her sweetheart, Giovanni Borrelli, when she was on holiday in Ischia three years ago.

Elfrida and their mother, Lady (Patricia) Eden, are in the island for the wedding. Amelia's father, Sir Timothy Eden, will not be here.

Lady Eden said she thought the journey, the heat and the crowds would be too much for him.

The people of Ischia are preparing to turn "their" wedding into the grandest fiesta they have ever seen.

The tiny village church at Basamiciola will be decorated with 2,000 white carnations.

Salute

A foghorn salute from all the ships in the harbour will greet the young couple as they leave the church. Among the wedding presents flowing into the island is a two-volume English-Italian language course—from the Italian professor who compiled it.

He is a complete stranger to Amelia and Giovanni.

One of the congratulatory cables was from Sir Anthony Eden and his wife. It said: "Lots of love and good wishes.— Anthony and Clarissa."

Tito Amilio, a famous Italian song writer, said today that he had written a special song for the wedding, called "L'Inglesina Innamorata"—the English Girl in Love.

They weren't serious!

Irene Dailey (top right) was the star of *Tomorrow – With Pictures*,
which sadly flopped.

98 Swan Court,
Chelsea, S.W.3.

20 July 1961.

Dear Elfrida Eden,

How strange that Michael Redgrave did not
answer - rather rude I call it, but I know he
is proverbially bad over letters!

Here is a letter to George Devine - send
it to him with a covering note from you. You
have done work in London, haven't you?

Let me know what happens. *good luck!*

Yours sincerely,

Sybil Thorndike

Sybil Thorndike did her best to help me

The article that lost me my job and
incurred the wrath of my father

Preparing for my part in *The Boyfriend*
at Hornchurch

In the press with
Dickie Henderson

ELFIE
FOR
THE U.S.

MISS ELFRIDA EDEN (above), 21-year-old actress niece of the Earl of Avon, is off to America early next year to try to break into television and the stage there.

Miss Eden tells me that it is on the advice of her mother, Lady Eden, wife of Sir Timothy, that she is going to New York. "She thought a year in the States would be good experience for me, so I am taking her advice," she says. "I have a few contacts there," she tells me, "and I shall also tour the acting studios.

"But I am now studying hard at shorthand and typing, so that I can take up secretarial work if I don't make it."

Miss Eden, who because of her height (5ft. 10in.) has had trouble in the past in getting acting parts, adds: "I am hoping that the men will be a bit taller in America."

My move to the US actually made the headlines!

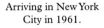

Arriving in New York City in 1961.

On top of the New World

Elfrida Eden finds the locals friendly

ENJOYING the view from the top: Miss Elfrida Eden, actress niece of the Earl of Avon, who has decided to take out American citizenship and seek stardom in the New World.

With my cameraman in New York she sat out on the roof of the 70-floor Rockefeller Centre. "I want to look at New York," she said. "This is the most exciting place in the world."

Though she is new to America—she has been there three days — she has a veteran's grasp of the country.

"Over here people are so friendly. You can go right to the top man and he will see you just like that." She snapped her fingers. "In London you make your appointments ages before, then hang around some agent's office for simply hours waiting to see him. Well, I just got tired of waiting."

And if, in spite of all those top people waiting to see her, success should elude Miss Eden? "Then I shall just live here and travel. I love America."

FOR A MOMENT ONLY, ELFRIDA EDEN TURNS HER BACK ON NEW YORK

I had the 'star' treatment when I arrived in New York

My father, aged 64

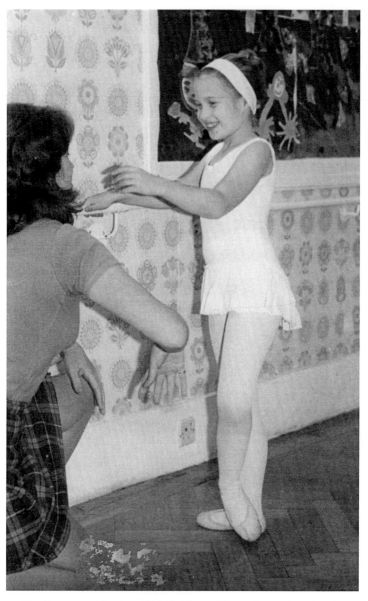

Teaching my goddaughter Michelle Morgan Witts, who graduated to the Rambert School before joining Vacani as a teacher.

I was so proud of my wedding present from my mother - a Ford Cortina

Wedding Day, 21/09/63, with Cristina and Emma Negretti, William Murray, Lucy Bethune and Philippa Stockley (l-r) and Charlotte and Emily Eden and Chiara Borrelli in front.

On board the
Cristoforo Colombo
during our honeymoon

Back in London
after my marriage

A moment of fun with Richard

Teaching at Lady Eden's - Lucy Bethune 2nd right front row,
next to my niece Emily Eden

With my friend David Jacobs

A Christmas visit from godfather David Jacobs

Suzy Says

A Party for Elfrida

ELFRIDA FALLOWFIELD (and if that isn't one of the all-time great Gothic-novel names), the daughter of the late Sir Timothy Eden, Baronet, and the niece of the Earl of Avon (Anthony Eden), stopped in Beverly Hills en route from London to Sydney with her husband, Richard.

Elfrida's cousin, Richard Gully, of the Hollywood branch of the family, gave a smallish dinner party for the Fallowfields at the Bistro, the Beverly Hills bunch's favorite hangout Among the guests were Merle Oberon and her fiance, Rob Wolders; Glenn Ford and his fiancee, Cynthia Hayward; Kathie and Darren McGavin, and Mrs. Robert Muir, an added starter on the Beverly Hills social scene.

Richard Fallowfield is the head of the advertising firm of Young & Rubicam in Australia, and Elfrida, who's terribly keen on ballet, has opened a ballet school in Sydney. Her brother, Sir John Eden, will be remembered as a cabinet minister in Edward Heath's recent government. It's a fancy family.

As for Mrs. Muir: Her husband, a multimillionaire, builds shopping centers all over the country. The Muirs live in a beautiful house in the Truesdale Estates area, and Mrs. Muir drives her own Rolls-Royce. She wants to be an actress. But, of course.

To get back to Elfrida for a moment—hers is a favorite family Christian name. Anthony Eden's mother, was called Marjorie. sister, who was also the Earl of Warwick's mother, was called Marjorie. Elfrida—although she preferred to use her second name, Marjorie always was a maverick.

Barbara Walters
She thought it was festive

It was an honour to be in Suzy's column in the New York Daily News!
A report of my Hollywood party

Family portrait by Tom Hustler, taken before we left for Australia

On holiday in Papua New Guinea – Richard, Tim, Laura, EE, Nick

Laura and Nick with baby crocodiles

Laura modelling, aged six

My mother's last birthday, 1990. EE, Rose, John, Ann and Amelia

Party for Betty Vacani when Mary and I became owners

Our first Vacani charity matinee in 1985 - scene from *Spring*

I dwarf Princess Margaret, who attended our matinee. Nikki Meinertzhagen, chairman of the charity committee, on my right

(photo Barry Swaebe).

Ex-Queen Anne-Marie of Greece with Princess Alexia (a Vacani pupil) and Prince Philippos, Guest of Honour at our fashion show.

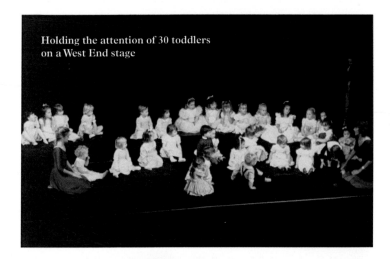

Holding the attention of 30 toddlers
on a West End stage

School is in step with a bygone age

winning." Although not a pupil, Princess Diana once worked there as an assistant.

When Miss Vacani retired, she handed the school over to two former pupils who moved to the basement of Debbie Moore's Pineapple Studio in Harrington Road.

Princess Beatrice used to attend classes, sometimes watched by her sister Eugenie. "Beatrice was a dear little girl," says Miss Eden, "But quite a monkey."

Princess Michael's children, Lord Frederick and Lady Gabriella; David Frost's sons; Peter de Savary's children and even Fifi Trixibelle, daughter of Paula Yates and Bob Geldof, have all tripped the light fantastic in the classes, which cost £65 a term.

The best testimony to the school's success comes from the mothers, who say: "If it's not a dancing day, we dare not walk past." So keen are the children to go down that inviting staircase.

Picture: DOUGLAS MORRIS

RHYTHM: Eager learners in class at the Vacani School

"Me and My Teddy Bear" - a class of two-year-olds with future
Team GB hurdler Lawrence Clarke (left) taking it seriously!

Mary Stassinopoulos and EE with Jo Holdsworth Hunt, Chairman of the Committee for our Leonora Fund fashion show.

With Dame Alicia Markova and Mary Stassinopoulos

CLARENCE HOUSE
SW1A 1BA

13th June 2000

Dear Mrs Eden

Thank you for your letter. I am so pleased to know that the Vacani School of Dancing has settled down well in its new home.

Queen Elizabeth The Queen Mother will be delighted that some of your children and their parents will be taking part in the Tribute on Horse Guards on Wednesday 19th July. I hope that the Producer, Major Michael Parker, is aware of your "surprise bouquet".

Yours sincerely

Private Secretary to
Queen Elizabeth The Queen Mother

Miss Elfrida Eden

A letter from our Patron

My debutante dress – modelled at Kensington Palace 50 years later!

Carefully touching the 'hot' water. A class of 3-4 year olds

Baby class at Vacani

Vacani brochure featuring Tamar Rafael and Chiara Vinci

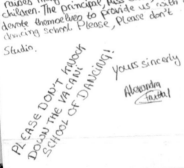

10 CHELSEA SQUARE
S.W.3
01-352 7708

22.2.95

To the council,

I am writting this letter on behalf of my dancing school 'Vacani'. Why on Earth do you want't knock down my wonderful dancing school to put up an OFFICE!? I am deeply raged. I have been going to Vacani since I was four years old; I am fourteen. This particular branch of the Vacani is very near to my home and I'm afraid that if it is knocked down, I might have to stop dancing completely as I am a fairly chubby child the dancing is very good for me, not only that but it is splendid and I enjoy it immensely. We'd put on a magnificent Matinee every two years in aid of the NSPCC and ICAN which raises many thousands of pounds for underprivileged children. The principal, Miss Eden, and the director, Miss Stone, devote themselves to provide us with a very special dancing school. Please, Please don't ...idestroy our Studio.

PLEASE DON'T KNOCK
DOWN THE VACANI
SCHOOL OF DANCING!

yours sincerly

Alexandra Fattal

Alexandra Fattal's letter trying to save our premises

Richard with Bridget Wrangham, helping us at the
Queen Mother's Birthday Parade

MUST-SEE TV

PICK OF THE DAY

Last Party At The Palace   Channel 4, 9pm

In 1958, a 200-year-old ceremony had its last hurrah: the presentation of aristocratic debutantes (debs) before the ruling monarch. It was, essentially, the scrapping of the upper-class's exclusive marriage market. This documentary looks at the lives of the last batch of taffeta-clad 'gells' who were expected to move seamlessly from the classroom to the altar via a four-month 'season' of parties, frocks and lunging chinless wonders.

In an age before tabloid 'It girls' and mass-market fashion, the extravagant showcase that made up 'the season' was documented by newspaper diarists and 'establishment bible' Tatler, as teenage girls, fresh out of their single-sex boarding schools, were thrust into a sink-or-swim social whirlpool that demanded they

of weeks. The idea that a woman could want more from life than a country pile or harbour any personal ambition of her own was unheard of. Out of that year's 1,400 debs (two of whom are above), only four went on to university.

The class of 1958 proved to be a mixed bag, however, and among those curtsying before the Queen that year were a future Marxist campaigner and even a thieving IRA sympathiser. With the radical ideals of the Sixties just around the corner, the debs' world of privilege and unchallenged deference was enjoying its last gasp, thanks partly to the infiltration of the nouveau riche to their blue-blooded ranks. Princess Margaret was heard to bemoan the ritual's demise by commenting regally: 'We had to put a stop to it, every tart in London was getting

Publicity for our
TV show, with
Fiona MacCarthy

Family evening - Tim, Juliet and Paula in front,
with Richard, EE, Nick and Laura standing.

Laura's wedding to Jamie Eynon, March 23rd 2013

With my Aunt Phil,
now 102!

In my Wiltshire garden
(photo by Alex Kennedy)

forms of dance, while continuing my acting and singing lessons. I knew my height was still a terrible drawback, but I had high hopes.

In September 1958, my darling sister Amelia married Giovanni Borrelli on the island of Ischia off Naples, Italy. This marriage engendered an enormous amount of publicity, as in those days it was still newsworthy for someone from our background to marry a person whose upbringing had been completely different.

Mia had to reside in Ischia for three weeks before her wedding, so I went with her. We were astonished to find ourselves followed every day by members of the press. Seemingly everyone on the island knew who we were, as they kept pointing us out and whispering. Ridiculous stories were printed about us, and rumours were flying that I too was engaged to an Italian! At last someone took charge and organised a daily press conference, on condition that we were left alone for the rest of the time.

Mummy and the rest of the family came out the week before the wedding, which was to be on September 7th. My sister had begged the Bishop of Ischia to allow her to have flowers and music in the church, as being a non-Catholic this normally was not allowed. She need not have bothered.

The only way we could get my beautiful sister into the church was by linking arms around her and kicking. The church was completely packed with islanders and tourists. People were standing on the pews and even overflowing onto the altar. All the time shouts of "*Auguri! Buona Fortuna!*" totally drowned out whatever music there might have been. The flowers were trampled on, or picked and thrown to the bride. The priest could hardly make himself heard over the cheerful noise whilst another member of the clergy stood in the pulpit taking photographs. Amelia looked shell-shocked, and we all stood around her protectively.

The service was, unsurprisingly, cut short. Giovanni and Amelia were then driven in an open car, followed by all of us, on a tour round the island. People had gathered by the sides of the roads, and they hurled sugared almonds at us, which hurt when they struck our heads!

What a relief to get to the hotel where the reception was held. The young couple left the island in a smart motor launch, and that evening a new song created in Amelia's honour was broadcast.

On the nearby island of Capri, another famous couple were being hounded by the press. This was none other than Elizabeth Taylor and Richard Burton.

The following year I went to Ischia again to stay with my sister, who was now expecting her first child. Once again it was rumoured that I would follow in her footsteps.

After all the excitement of Mia's wedding I returned to London and did my best to find work in the theatre. Always being short of money, I took whatever job I could in the meantime. I continued to work in the school as well as getting many jobs as a baby sitter and even a cleaner. I did think it was a bit incongruous one day when my brother had invited me to the Opening of Parliament, which I attended in all my finery, to find myself a few hours later, still in my hat, negotiating a fire-escape staircase which led to the apartment of four scruffy young men who employed me as their cleaner!

I wrote to every theatre I could think of asking to be an ASM (assistant stage manager) and applied to every advertising agency in London asking for an audition. I did manage to get some TV commercials, and they certainly kept the wolf from the door and gave me much-needed experience.

During 1959 I managed to find more theatrical work, mainly on television. Two Children's Hour series kept me happily busy for some months and gave me my first taste of working on location.

Despite the fact that I had been a debutante the previous year, I found I was still asked to parties and events, and was finally chosen to take part in a fashion show, so I learned how to walk as a model. I was also asked to be chairman of a charity dance which I found too much like hard work!

My days were filled with teaching at Lady Eden's School, attending ballet, drama and singing classes and every so often finding work on TV. In the evenings I was often taken out to theatres, dinners and eventually night clubs like the Blue Angel, the 400 or Quaglino's.

Rumours were still circulating that I too would marry an Italian, and one day a reporter I knew from Mia's wedding appeared at my door and scooped me up, taking me to lunch before going to his offices to write an article, and finishing with dinner and a night club. This was to keep me away from other reporters. It worked, as when I finally went home I realised another journalist had waited six hours to interview me before he gave up!

On my father's side I had a remarkable cousin called Richard Gully. Richard was born a couple of months before his parents were married, and this was in the days when such things mattered; had he been acknowledged as the eldest son, he would have inherited a title. As it was, he had to suffer the ignominy of seeing his younger brother succeed in his place.

Richard came into my life when I was 18 and seriously

trying to get some work in the theatre. I knew his lovely sister, Signe Brandon, very well, but Richard was an unknown – luckily, not for long. Despite the fact that he lived in California and I was in England, we began a friendship that lasted until his death some forty-odd years later.

Richard was tall, debonair and every inch the perfect English gentleman. However, he made the decision that if he could not be a viscount, he might as well be an actor. He persuaded our other cousin, Fulke, heir to the Earl of Warwick, to go with him to Hollywood to break into the emerging world of films.

Thanks to their good looks and lovely English accents, Richard and Fulke were offered work at once. Alas, Fulke proved a disaster as an actor, and while Richard was better, he found himself fascinated by the film world from the other side of the camera. Fulke returned to England, while Richard was taken on by Jack Warner as his right-hand man, a position he occupied for many very successful years. During this time not only did Richard come into contact with all the famous film stars of the day, he met some notorious gangsters, people who obviously had some sway in Hollywood. Richard was quite unfazed, although this was a somewhat far cry from his extremely proper English upbringing. Years later he said to me, "Lucky Luciano was a most charming fellow. It was hard to believe he had instigated the murder of so many people."

Richard was a wonderful correspondent. He would send me exciting, fat letters containing copies of the column he wrote in a weekly newspaper. He would write about me at every available opportunity and loved the fact that we were cousins. He knew anyone of any importance in Hollywood, and everyone wanted to know him.

Richard introduced me to the actor Robert Wagner when

he was making a film in England. Robert W was a total delight. He was also extremely attractive, and was kindness itself to me, thanks once again to my dear cousin Richard. I was invited to Pinewood studios, and when Robert was working, I sat in his special chair. In between takes we chatted, and he wanted to know all about my life and my relationship with Richard Gully. It was so dreadful some years later when his wife, Natalie Wood, tragically drowned. Natalie was enchanting, and it seems the mystery still remains unsolved, though disquieting rumours abound.

George Hamilton invited me to lunch at the Savoy, and 1 was bowled over by his good looks. Richard also arranged for me to meet several film producers and casting agents. Unfortunately 1 was so unworldly and so 'ballet trained' that 1 was not able to take advantage of these marvellous introductions. I was still really a very naïve young girl.

CHAPTER TWELVE

THE NAME'S BOND...

On reflection my life was an extraordinary mixture. One moment I was the lowest dogsbody school teacher or cleaner, the next a serious student of dance and theatre, and finally I found myself being treated like a celebrity. No wonder I was sometimes rather confused.

This weird existence continued all through 1960. I mainly lived in London, and was quite pleased to get as much work as I did, even though the parts were often very small. I appeared in The Dickie Henderson Show as a freakishly tall Geisha girl, which recalled the time I had danced with Norman Wisdom at a ball some months before. I found Norman Wisdom as funny in real life as he was on the screen. He had such an amusing face.

He thought it hilarious that I was so much taller than him, but he was an excellent dancer, and we enjoyed ourselves at the ball. He said he would like me to appear in one of his films, and true to his word, a short time later I received an invitation to meet the producer. I was so excited, but it was not to be. My dear dancing teacher Enid said to my mother, "Oh you can't let Elfie go and work with Norman Wisdom, he is a horrid little man." I wish my mother had not listened to her, as I lost the opportunity to gain some valuable experience. I also thought it was rather unkind.

I had a wonderful time working for the Repertory Players. This was a professional group of actors and authors who staged plays in London theatres on Sunday nights. I was ASM and then Deputy Stage Manager on two plays written by Hubert Gregg. He was a delightful man and the experience he gave me was invaluable.

I was most excited to be given the job of ASM at the Apollo Theatre in London during a review called *Pieces Of 8,* starring Kenneth Williams and Fenella Fielding. At last I was associated with a West End production, and I loved every minute of it. Kenneth Williams was a strange man. He never mixed with the rest of the cast, and studiously ignored us when we all had a meal between shows on matinee days. He didn't like me, and called me "that silly little deb girl". Even so, he made me laugh every night. He could be unkind though and used to sneer at the audience as he descended from the gods dressed as an angel as he could make them laugh so easily.

It was during my time with *Pieces of 8* that I qualified and enrolled as a member of Equity, the Actors' Union. Now I was a professional!

I had a great rapport with the backstage staff. They were

divided into stage hands and prop boys. They called me Charlie (from my second name) and we used to exchange banter and jokes all evening. Alas, one day I committed a cardinal sin. I was leading Kenneth off the stage during a blackout when I saw he was about to be hit on the head by a balloon. I knew he would make my life miserable if it had touched him, so I grabbed it and handed it to the nearest person to me. Unfortunately this was a stagehand and not a prop boy. When I had returned from Kenneth's dressing room the entire backstage staff was on strike. They sat with faces of thunder, until I apologised. At first I laughed, as I thought they were joking, but they were deadly serious. So I grovelled – and they returned to work. I didn't feel quite the same about them after that.

In May 1960 I was actually offered a speaking part in a play which was to tour and then end up in the West End. It was called *Tomorrow With Pictures*. I was more than excited, although the part was minor in the extreme. The play starred Irene Dailey and Conrad Phillips, who later became famous for playing William Tell on television. Unfortunately the play had two authors, and neither wanted his words cut. At the end of the first night in Brighton we were booed, as it ran for over three hours. The authors fought all the next day, and the atmosphere was dreadful.

At last an agreement was reached, and the first part to be cut – was mine! Everyone was sorry for me, as they knew how thrilled I had been to get the part. Irene then offered me the job of being her dresser, for £6 per week. The authors then said I could have a walk-on part and understudy another actress, also for £6 per week, which made up my salary. In the event I stayed the course until the bitter end, as gradually other parts were cut. One night the actress I was understudying pretended to be ill so I could go on in her place. This was my one and only speaking appearance as an actress in the West End.

When we had finally opened at the Duke of York's Theatre in St Martin's Lane the brand new musical *Oliver* was playing to packed houses in the next-door theatre. One of my jobs was to approach people in the queues and entice them to watch our play instead by offering them "twofers". What a contrast for those people expecting to see the hit musical to have to watch Irene searching desperately for her pills with dramatic cries, all in a nearly empty theatre!

Also starring in *Tomorrow With Pictures* was a young actor called James Villiers. James and I became very close. He took it upon himself to teach me to be more sophisticated, and made me wear tight skirts. Until then I had worn full skirts, as I thought they would make me look less tall. He made me practise walking – but not like a ballet dancer!

Jimmy was very stern with me, but I fell totally in love with him. He gave me a beautiful Siamese kitten, which we called Binky after Binky Beaumont. Binky (my Binky) was a tremendous character and was more like a dog than a cat. I would take him everywhere with me on a collar and lead, even to the park, where he loved to climb trees until I called him back. Every night I took him to the theatre. I shinned up the fire escape, where a fellow cast member took him through a window, and collected him the same way at the end of the show. We would then meet Jimmy in the pub across the road, where Binky and the resident dog proceeded to entertain everyone with their antics and wild games.

Thanks to my friendship with Jimmy I met many wonderful actors, most of whom had been at RADA with him, and all of whom became famous - Peter O'Toole, Peter Bowles, Ronnie Fraser, Georgia Brown, Paddy Newell and Bryan Pringle, to name a few.

My parents liked Jimmy, although my father expressed a few anxieties. It all seemed too good to be true, and it was. Sadly there was a problem, in the shape of a bottle – or three. Jimmy sober was a delight. The other Jimmy was not, and I was too young and inexperienced to know how to cope. Our romance came to an end, and I was devastated.

Around this time Ronald Fraser and his wife (Ronnie called me 'the schoolteacher"!) invited me to a party. I knew Jimmy would be there, and thought that with luck our romance could be rekindled. I chose my clothes with care, and wore a new shirt in a bright colour. It was in fact a man's shirt, and I had bought three, as I thought they were particularly snazzy.

The party was in full swing when I arrived. The Peters, O'Toole and Bowles, were talking together with dear Bryan Pringle and Paddy Newell. Then I spied Jimmy, chatting to Georgia Browne. It was a star-studded event, but my main concern was that I was being ignored by the object of my desire.

Just as I was wondering what to do about this, the door burst open and in came an actor I recognised as Sean Connery, a big, dark, impressive-looking man. His handsome face wore a grin from ear to ear. "I've just landed the part of James Bond!" he announced to the assembled company, and we all whooped and cheered and congratulated him on this success. Little did we know just how big a name Sean was to become.

About half way through the party I found myself talking to him. I had not met him before, but I thought he was extremely attractive. Amazingly enough, he appeared to like me too. Yet out of the corner of my eye I was still looking for Jimmy. Could he see me? Did he realise I was talking to James Bond? Surely he would be jealous and come over and join us? But no, he continued to behave as if I simply wasn't there. Seeing this, I must confess that I began to flirt outrageously with the man who was about to become 007, the most famous spy in the world.

"I like your shirt" he said.

"Oh do you?" I replied. "It's a man's shirt actually, and I have two more at home."

"Would you give me one?"

"Of course" I said, "When would you like it?"

"What's wrong with now?" was the somewhat surprising answer.

"Of course" I said. He took my hand, and we surreptitiously left the party.

Oh the naivety, the stupidity, the folly of youth! 1 truly believed that when Sean Connery took me home it was just because he wanted one of my shirts. But all I could think about was that I wanted the original James, the man 1 was crazy about. I wanted him to know that someone else found me attractive so that perhaps he would come back and claim me.

I opened my front door and Sean stepped inside. Only our lovely housekeeper, Anna, was there, and I was sure she was sound asleep at such a late hour. I scooted happily upstairs to find the other two shirts and brought them down for Sean.

"Oh you silly girl!" this soon-to-be very famous actor said. "Did you honestly think 1 was really interested in your shirts?"

What an incredible little fool I felt! Sean was making it quite clear what he really wanted from me, and I had to make it equally clear that I did not feel the same way. I confess there was a slight tussle, but then Sean accepted that I meant what I said. After that, thank goodness, he was enormously gracious. He said that never before had he met a girl whose mind was stronger than her body. He assured me there were no hard feelings before he bade me good night and left. I sat miserably alone, caressing a somewhat smarting cheek (Paris, Switzerland and now London!) and realising how stupidly I had behaved.

But the night's adventures were not over. Just then there came a tentative knock on the door. It was Anna. With tears in her eyes, she told me that my darling little Binky had run into the road, straight under the wheels of a car, and was dead. The driver knew Binky and was almost as upset as I was.

I was beside myself with grief. This very special little cat had been adored by so many people. In the letter Hubert Gregg had written to me after his play he said, "Work for me again, and please bring Binky!"

I rang Jimmy at once, and he sweetly came straight away and did his best to comfort me. He could not have been kinder, but he made it clear, gently but firmly, that our romance was over.

When at last I fell asleep that night my pillow was sodden with tears. Tears for my precious Binky, and many more for my lost love. James Villiers was a good actor and an extremely funny man. We rekindled our friendship many years later, and my husband thoroughly enjoyed his company.

★ ★ ★

Around this time I was excited at being granted an interview for a part in a television drama at the BBC. On arrival I was a bit surprised to find myself in a small office alone with the producer. After an initial talk, he asked to see my legs. Gingerly I lifted up my skirt. That was not good enough! Up on the table I had to clamber in order for this man to seriously check my legs and confirm that I did indeed have two!

The top I was wearing was apparently too concealing. I refused to take it off, but I had to pull it behind my back to show that I had two of those as well!

I was then required to read the part. It was a love scene, and Mr P read the male part as he sat on the other side of the desk. He then declared that this was no good, so he moved next to me. When it came to the passionate kiss, I decided the part was not worth it – and escaped!

In 1961, having written close to 100 letters, I received a positive reply from the theatre in Hornchurch, Essex. To my joy I was being offered parts in pantomime, with even a small speaking part as the Queen of Saramond in *Sinbad The Sailor*.

Finally I had some positive news to give to the mad journalists who constantly rang me. The resulting publicity was good for the theatre, and undoubtedly due to my clever uncle I was then offered a good part in the first production out of the West End of *The Boy Friend* by Sandy Wilson. I was in my element! The dancing was a piece of cake, and the Charleston is one of my favourite dances. I could manage the singing, and during this production I realised I had a gift for comedy. The management were extremely happy at the extra publicity, and even I didn't mind the headline in one paper which read "LAST OF THE DEBS SAYS "I'LL HAVE A BITTER".

The Boy Friend became a great favourite of mind and in subsequent years I produced it on more than one occasion.

Telling journalists what I was doing lost me a really good job a short while later. I had won a part, entirely on my own with no strings being pulled, in a series of TV advertisements with Hughie Green. I was meant to be an air hostess, and I used the name Charlotte Grey. Stupidly I told a newspaper, and when it appeared the next day I was in deep trouble. First I lost the job, and the company then used a real air hostess who could not act, but even worse for me was the utter fury of my father, who accused me of dragging his mother's name (Grey) through the "mud and slime of the gutter press". A salutary lesson.

CHAPTER THIRTEEN

FIRST BITE OF THE BIG APPLE

When I was growing up in London, I remember occasional visits to Piccadilly with my mother (maybe with a special treat of an ice cream soda at Fortnum and Mason – or shopping in Bond Street), and gazing at all the photographs that were displayed in the windows of the Cunard Line offices of the well-known people who had arrived from the USA on board one of the great passenger ships of the day, the *Queen Mary* or the *Queen Elizabeth*. Famous people from stage, screen and business, posed in their minks and their little hats or their homburgs and overcoats casually draped over shoulders, clutching beauty boxes or brief cases, and sometimes holding the lead of a miniature poodle, or the hand of a cutely-dressed child. These people fascinated me, and I longed to be one of them. Once home we would listen to *In Town Tonight!* on the wireless, and hear some of these stars being interviewed.

I had been very lucky to have visited New York on two occasions with my mother to stay with my Aunt Phil. New York City was a magical place for me. Sparkling, energetic, so exciting and so utterly different from drab, grey, post-war London.

NYC had 'drug stores' which sold amazing ice cream sodas. The shops were full of clothes and merchandise which was a million times removed from the utilitarian objects which were displayed in our shops.

I don't think I stopped smiling on my visit to this city when I was 11 years old, from the first moment I picked out the Statue of Liberty from the deck of our ship, as it emerged from the early morning greeny-grey darkness.

The top of the Empire State Building – WOW! I couldn't drink in enough of the excitement that was laid before me. Radio City Music Hall… the very words engulfed me with joyous anticipation. How amazing to see a film (sorry, movie!) and a stage show as well. I gazed with awe and admiration at the precision and brilliance of the Rockettes with their seemingly endlessly long legs. The Roxy had been almost as exciting, especially when the lights dimmed at the start of the show and the skyline of NYC appeared all round the top of the theatre against a darkening and finally star-filled sky.

Now, at the age of 21, it was agreed that I would go to live in New York for a while. I was almost beside myself with excitement, not least because it meant (or so I thought) that I would be my own boss, and would be able to make my own decisions, good or bad. I had planned and plotted for this event for years, and could hardly believe I was eventually being allowed to go. For several years I had had the strongest conviction that I would meet my future husband in New York City.

For my 21st birthday my mother had sweetly given me a room in our house in Victoria Road. She had decorated it and filled it with furniture, pictures and ornaments, all of which were meant to be mine. I had a beautiful baby grand piano, and although never a very accomplished pianist, I played this by the hour, and occasionally friends would be happy to listen to me.

I truly loved this room, and my mother let me entertain there whenever I wanted. It was, though, still 'at home' and I longed to spread my wings and be independent.

My decision to leave London had been strongly influenced by a disappointment in my career. I had a theatrical agent by this time, and one day he informed me I was to be in a film in which I would have a large part. The producers said they saw me as a future Kay Kendall (an actress I had long admired), and the words "introducing Elfrida Eden" would be on the credits. I could hardly believe my good fortune, and rushed off to Spain on holiday to celebrate. Ah, woe is me! Once again I experienced a massive letdown. A few months later I was told that sadly the film had been shelved. New York was the obvious answer. I needed to get away.

Living in the USA for a while seemed a very exciting opportunity. I found a teacher of typing and shorthand, and made a good start, although I never finished the course. Armed with an amazing lack of qualifications but untold enthusiasm, I felt sure I would succeed in the Big Apple. A journalist somehow heard this news and printed a perfectly acceptable article in the *Sunday Express* headed "ELFIE FOR THE US".

The days leading up to my departure on board the SS *United*

States were filled with nerves and second thoughts. I was very sad at saying goodbye to my father. I did not know I would never see him again.

The ship was a day late docking at Southampton, due to dreadful weather conditions when she left New York. The entire complement of Fritham House School, girls, staff and domestic staff lined up to say goodbye to me. It was dreadful saying goodbye to Mummy and suddenly I did not want to go at all.

I had a cabin to myself, and it was filled to overflowing with flowers, telegrams and cards from friends and family. I went up on deck, and leaning over the rail, I was able to spot Mummy and my sister. I threw a streamer, and Amelia caught it.

The noise of impending departure gained momentum. Sirens sounded the "All Visitors Ashore" signal. Hoots and clangs intermingled with shouts from passengers to friends on the quay, as suddenly, almost imperceptibly, we eased away from the dock, and my streamer broke.

I stood on deck waving until I could see no more through my tears, and then I returned to my cabin to open my messages and gaze at my flowers.

The crew were all exhausted, as they had had to endure a quick turnaround with no day off in between. They were therefore thoroughly bad tempered, and not the least bit like the wonderful people who had looked after us on the *Queen Elizabeth*.

The first night out at sea was horrendously rough. I was trying to sleep in my little cabin, but one minute we were floating endlessly up to the heavens, and the next minute crashing deeper and ever deeper down into the waves. Despite the stabilisers we suffered a serious amount of rolling as well. After one particularly spectacular crash, I found myself drenched in water. My immediate thought was that the porthole had burst open, and I lay there expecting to drown. When I didn't, a furtive exploration with my hands discovered that like Ophelia, I was lying in water surrounded by flowers! I was alive – but wet.

On arrival In New York, I found myself treated like a celebrity. To my amazement there was a mass of photographers all wanting me to pose for them. They perched me up on a rail with the New York skyline behind and took photos which appeared in several newspapers the next day. Added to this I was interviewed by Gabe Pressman, who had radio and TV shows, and it was said to be a great honour to be on his programme. So a dream had come true – and I was one of the people interviewed on the equivalent show of *In Town Tonight*.

Slightly bemused by all this, but terribly excited, I was brought back to earth with a bump when I was severely ticked off by my aunt, who had been waiting for me with her friend Monie with growing impatience. They had not been allowed on board, and I was about the last to disembark. Not an auspicious start!

I had, of course, travelled with a trunk of clothes. This was immediately unpacked by Phil and Monie with cries of derision and horror at the inappropriate contents. I was upset, as Mummy and I had packed with great care, and thought we had done rather well.

Mummy had given me some money which was meant to last me until I found a job. She reckoned without Auntie. On my first day in New York I was dragged off to the shops, where Filly enjoyed herself spending my money. It seemed to run in the family, this enjoyment of my mother and my aunt in spending money that was not theirs!

The first purchase she made me buy – essential, I was assured

- was a severely-boned black lace corset and suspender belt in one, trimmed with pink. It cost a fortune. I can say now, without any false modesty, that I had a perfect figure with a 23" waist and positively no need for a corset. A good dress and some hideous shoes followed, and together they ensured I had no money left to tide me over.

Next on the agenda was finding a job. Auntie decided to help. She introduced me to a friend of hers called Bob, who arranged for me to work in a Jewish law firm in the Wall Street area of Manhattan.

I was horrified. I had no interest in law, and the last thing I wanted was to work in a company such as this. The immediate problem was that I couldn't understand a word they said. I had only just arrived in New York, and the strong Jewish-American accent defeated me. The legal terms they used were also seemingly in another language, and the typing they expected me to do bore no correlation to the genteel "Dear Sir" letters I had been practising in England.

As if all this wasn't bad enough, I had to take over from the switchboard operator during her lunch break. I sat before this huge board with a mass of wires and sockets, with not the faintest clue of what I was meant to do. This, combined with the fact that I mixed up Mr Feisselbaum with Mr Henkelstuck, did not endear me to my bosses.

At the end of the day, the entire company left the office and told me to close up and lock the doors. I did just that. I posted the keys through the door, and vowed never to return.

"Why did you leave?" my aunt enquired. "Bob said they loved you!"

My dear aunt decided to accompany me to an employment agency the next day. When I was called for my interview, Auntie insisted on coming in with me.

"Can you type, honey?" I was asked.

"Yes she can, and very well too" Auntie replied before I had a chance.

"Enough already," I said to myself, already picking up the lingo. "Next time I go alone."

One of my few talents is my ability to mimic. I have a "good ear" and can pick up languages very quickly, and fool people who don't know into thinking I can actually speak quite well. This enabled me to secure a job as a guide at the Rockefeller Centre. It was essential that guides could speak at least two languages, and I trotted out my well-rehearsed sentences in French, German and Italian which, combined with my "lovely English accent", did the trick.

I found it rather like being back at school. Our boss was just like a strict headmistress, and there were the 'goody goody' girls who spoke brilliant languages and were perfect guides, and there were the naughty ones like me.

To start with I sat behind a desk with a sign which announced that I could speak French, German and Italian. I was terrified in case anyone asked me anything in one of these, and the tourists must have been surprised at my appallingly bad replies to their queries.

My aunt's friend Bob had introduced me to an extremely weird man with almost white blonde hair. He took a fancy to me, and I found him decidedly spooky and far too old for me. One day Bob told my aunt that I was invited out for an evening, and asked me to wear the blue dress that had been bought for me on my first day. As soon as I arrived at the meeting place I saw this weird man talking to Bob, and before I knew it, Bob had left me alone with him.

Luckily I have no recollection of his name. I shall call him

Spook. He took me out to dinner, and of course I was polite and answered his questions, as that was how I had been brought up. He was considerably older than I.

Spook drove me back through Central Park, when he suddenly veered off into a hidden parking place. The next instant I found myself practically flat on my back, as he had caused the seat I was in to recline. Immediately he was on top of me, and trying to get into my dress. It was at this instant that I thanked Auntie for choosing this dress, as it was made in two parts, and the under part was extremely tight, and luckily for me this ghastly man could make no progress!

I fought him off, and insisted he take me home. He did, but he didn't give me up. He discovered where I was working and one day he hovered, leeringly, by the little desk I was manning, completely unnerving me. What a lucky chance it was that my brother was visiting New York that very day, and had popped in to see me. He gave Spook short shrift, and I am happy to say I never saw him again.

I did adore my aunt and we had enormous fun together, even if she did at times try to run my life for me. I felt it was time to find somewhere of my own to live and to this end I decided to contact a new friend I had made in London.

Jean Callender (Bird) and I shared an apartment together in NYC, and at last I discovered the joy of sharing a flat and living a totally free life. We shared with two American girls, and all four of us became the closest of friends. The apartment was in Greenwich Village, and it was one of the happiest places I have live in.

We had crazy times – and some interesting adventures. Helen Gurley Brown's book *Sex And The Single Girl* had just come out and we devoured it, eager to learn the tricks of the trade. We decided to give a brunch party one Sunday, and concocted the utterly delicious and totally lethal iced coffee drink that was featured in the book. An entire bottle of vodka was required, along with six cups of extremely strong coffee and a quart of the best vanilla ice cream. It was the hugest success and Jean and I laugh about it to this day as we recall those happy, somewhat tipsy young men!

At this time I also changed my job. I marched into some offices on the 45th floor of the RCA building, still dressed in my guide's uniform, to answer an advertisement for a 'Gal Friday' to work for an oil company, a very small subsidiary of Standard Oil of California. For some unknown reason they gave me the job.

What a happy time this was! I was completely useless at everything, but they loved me, and I loved them. My gorgeous boss, Frank, had never met anyone quite like me before. One day I played a cruel trick on him. I had in my possession a hairpiece of exactly my own colour. Beehive hairstyles had been popular when I was a deb, and the use of hairpieces was common. On this particular occasion I arrived with the hairpiece artfully concealed in my own hair. The rest of the office were in on the joke and were hiding by Frank's office.

I went into Frank's office for dictation, and begged him not to go too fast. He duly slowed down, but I went into hysterics, and cried it was much too fast and I couldn't cope, and he looked up to see me apparently pulling out a huge clump of my own hair. Poor man, he practically had a fit!

Before Christmas we all went out to lunch, and I decided that as I was in Manhattan, I would drink Manhattans. Whoops – I didn't realise this was a bourbon-based cocktail, and I am afraid the rest of the day passed off in a foggy haze of misery as I tried to recover on the sofa in the Chairman's office.

Jean had also started a new job, at McCann Erickson, the advertising agency, where she became a very successful art director. After her first day in this new job, Jean told me about an Englishman who had breezed into her office to welcome her. Being English, tall and extremely good-looking, this young man, Dick Fallowfield, was obviously used to the fall-about attention he received from the young American girls in the agency.

We then discovered that another friend of ours, Maggie McKay (Chilton), had dated Dick for a while, but he had given her a bit of a run-around, so we decided that it was time for Dick to be given a taste of his own medicine. As he had never met me, I was the person chosen to teach him a lesson.

On Thursday 6th December 1962 I was unaware that my premonition had come true. We had been invited to Maggie's farewell party before she returned to England. Dick was there, and he was pointed out to me on arrival. I studiously ignored him. I flirted outrageously with his flatmates, and when he begged for my telephone number, I told him only that I worked for a subsidiary company of Standard Oil of California. In those days there were thirty-five such companies in New York, and ours, California Commercial Company, was the smallest of the lot.

After the party we giggled at the thought of how I would tease him. I did not admit to my friends that secretly I thought he really was rather a dish.

Occasionally I had to relieve the receptionist, and I quite enjoyed this, as everyone remarked on my accent. The best one was when I had replied, "I am so sorry, I am afraid Mr Joyce is out. May I give him a message?" The reaction from the caller was "You're *sarry*? You're *afraid*? Oh Gahd, I LOVE it!"

Just before the end of the working day on the Monday after

the party, I answered the telephone, and it was Dick, who had ploughed his way through all thirty-five companies to find me! Of course I agreed to go out with him after that, and our first date was to see *Aida* at the Met in New York, which was totally wonderful.

This production was memorable in many ways. Because of the snow in Washington, the tenor, Franco Corelli, was unable to appear. At the very last minute a young American tenor stepped in, but he only knew the opera in German, while the rest of the cast sang in Italian. The first aria, 'Celeste Aida', was fine – Italian – but when he then burst into guttural German, the entire audience fell about laughing. Poor young man. He struggled on, and we soon became used to it.

Dick and I started dating seriously, and we began to discover how much we had in common. We survived a dreadful trip to the country, where we were completely snowbound, had nothing to eat and were utterly miserable. Christmas was approaching, and I was of course due to spend it with my aunt and her friends, Monie and Frank. Dick told me he had nowhere to go, so of course I asked if he could join us. My aunt and Monie obviously liked Dick very much and I found my feelings for him were becoming serious. However, I was somewhat surprised, although very pleased, when he told me on Boxing Day that he wanted to marry me! I would not let him ask me for a while, as I thought it would be a good idea to get to know him a bit better.

Apart from the fact that Dick was extremely handsome, it was soon apparent that we were on the same wavelength. We shared a similar sense of humour. He was definitely someone with whom I could behave idiotically and have enormous fun. Love of animals and the countryside was so important to me, and I was delighted to find he felt the same. Essential as all that was for me, Dick was also a very kind man. He had lost his parents when he was still young, and I could tell he was longing for his own family.

CHAPTER FOURTEEN

LOVE AND LOSS

I made Richard wait until 16th January 1963 before I accepted his proposal. I found it hard to believe it had happened quite so quickly. For the ensuing weeks I wafted about in a haze of happiness. Together we found another apartment, although of course he did not live there as we weren't married yet, so Jean came to share it with me. Jean had the bedroom, and I slept on a sofa bed in the little sitting room on the top floor, only five floors up.

One night I had gone to sleep in my usual position with my head towards the window when there was a dreadful thunderstorm. After one particularly huge clap of thunder and bolt of lightning, there was a horrendous sound of crashing and breaking glass, and I was sure a plane had crashed onto the roof above my head. I screamed loudly and quickly pulled the bedclothes over my head, which undoubtedly saved my life. Once again, as on board ship, I tentatively felt around when the noise had somewhat subsided. I was surrounded by shards of broken glass, and on my pillow just millimetres from my head was the top of an enormous wooden pole which had been positioned between all our apartments at the back. This pole was used to attach washing lines to each flat and had obviously been struck by lightning.

I reflected on how close I had come on three occasions to death from breaking windows. The first from the bomb in Albert Hall Mansions, the second, not really a danger though it felt it at the time, on the ship, and finally in my little New York apartment.

After I had accepted his proposal, Dick wrote to my father to ask his permission to marry me. For some reason, I had also decided to let my father in on the secret before I told my mother. I received a wonderful letter from him, delighted at the news. I had admitted to him that my only worry was that Elfrida did not go very well with Fallowfield. As my father had changed Mummy's name when they married, I thought he might suggest an alternative for me. Instead I received the following poem, which he had written for fun:

ELFIN MAGIC
Oh, fallow, fallow lay the field
Till Elfie came along!
No blade could sprout, no ear could yield –
Oh, fallow, fallow lay the field
And sad the reaper's song!

But blithely sprang the young green corn,
And loud the laughter peal'd
When Eden's Garden one gay morn,
Became a Fallowfield.

Soon after I had received this letter on May 13th 1963, my aunt appeared at my apartment door, and I immediately knew something dreadful had happened. She stood there unable to speak, but her face said it all. My father had died suddenly of a heart attack at home in the New Forest, in my mother's arms.

I flew back to England for the funeral. This was the first time I had crossed the Atlantic by air. My sister Rose met me, and we realised we hadn't seen each other for seven years.

Daddy was lying in his coffin in his beautiful library dressed in his favourite plum velvet smoking jacket. I gazed at his familiar face, so still and lifeless, and longed to tell him how much I loved his poem and please could he change his mind and not be dead, and instead be there to give me away at my wedding.

His service was so moving. All the girls from the school were there, and my brother gave a wonderful address. It was a perfect spring day and Mummy was in her element organising the myriads of flowers around the grave into whatever order she wanted.

I loved my father, and was only sad that he didn't really get to know me in adult life, when he would have discovered how like him I was, and how I shared his sentiments and thoughts so much. I missed him dreadfully.

By the time Richard received Daddy's reply to his letter, I was already in England for his funeral. Luckily he had given his permission, and said how much he was looking forward to meeting his future son-in-law.

★ ★ ★

On my return to New York, my feelings were a mixture of sadness about my father and happy anticipation about my forthcoming marriage. I designed the dresses for the bridesmaids and sent the drawing to England. Richard had told me all his cousins' children would be too young to take part, so I chose eight from my side. Big black mark! There were several children who would have been eligible, and I had a bit of a hill to climb with his relations due to that decision. Richard's parents being dead, his closest relative was his sister Julie. Richard's family were English/Scottish, and his mother, her two sisters and their husbands had all ended up living in Sri Lanka, then known as Ceylon. The family had one or two preconceived ideas about me, and one of them was that I was Roman Catholic, as R. had told his sister by letter that he had taken me to Mass at the weekend. But it was Mass as in Massachusetts and not church!

Mummy planned to come to New York to meet Richard and do some shopping, but the day before she was due to come she had to cancel, as she was unwell. I had no idea what was wrong with her, but I felt it was serious. She came a few weeks later, and although she was frail, the fun of being in New York City and being with me, Richard and her sister, soon made her feel much better – and the shopping began!

Brilliantly, we found my wedding dress at Bergdorf Goodman. A beautiful dress, which luckily, as so many of my possessions went missing, I was able to keep. I hated to see Mummy go when she returned to England, and decided then and there to surprise her by returning home earlier than she expected.

I had been given a wonderful present - to return to the UK First Class aboard a new French liner called the SS *France*. I hated to forgo this luxury, but I did, and instead returned Cabin Class on the SS *United States* again. As the ship slowly pulled away from the dock to the sounds of a lone set of bagpipes playing *Speed Bonny Boat,* I was up on the deck and looking towards the RCA building. Suddenly a huge sheet fluttered out of the window 45 floors up – and I knew my dear friends in California Commercial Company were dangerously leaning out of the window and waving as they called out (so I learned later) "Bon voyage – and good luck!"

I thoroughly enjoyed the journey and was extremely spoilt. I sat at the Purser's table with some fascinating people, including an elderly American lady from the Mid-West who had learned to shoot a target while riding at full gallop when she was only six! I was called 'The Bride of the Equinox' and they were all absolutely charming to me.

Two days before we docked, Mummy was given my letter telling her I would soon be with her. She met me at Southampton and couldn't wait to rush me home to show me my wedding present. It was a beautiful new Ford Cortina, white with a red interior. I couldn't believe it - my very own car! For the next two weeks Mummy and I drove all over the place visiting friends and relations, and of course, shopping.

I was not a very experienced driver. Before I met Richard I had borrowed a boyfriend's rather snazzy two-seater convertible, and actually managed to follow the words of the song by becoming stuck in the grooves on the 59th Street Bridge!

When Richard arrived for our wedding I met him at the

airport, and we were besieged by photographers. Next day under one of the photos in the paper the caption read, "Mr Fallowfield was shown his fiancée's new car – 'Gee honey!' he said, 'That sure is swell!' They had assumed he was American.

Our wedding was lovely – on the whole. Mummy organised everything, and I barely knew half the guests. A busload of domestic staff and helpers came up from Fritham, and rather more substantial food such as pork pies and beer was prepared for them in one of the rooms. Somehow Richard's family found their way to this room and thought these were the only eats provided. Sadly they never found the deliciousness from Gloriette, and we later heard comments about the less than delicate food on offer!

Richard drove me away in my pretty car and as he rounded the corner, he was on the wrong side of the road. Our marriage very nearly ended then and there, as we almost collided head-on with a huge lorry.

Our first night was spent, as my father had arranged, in the Savoy Hotel. There was a sunken bath in our 'en suite' and it was huge. As I got into it I slipped right under the water, ruining my perfect Renée-created hair!

Our honeymoon involved taking an Italian liner back to NYC via the southern route, which took ten days. We were first class this time and therefore at the Captain's table. Also at this table were a couple who became instant friends, Anne and Geoff Mytton, and a very amusing Italian gentleman called Renzo Olivieri. We had a brilliant time, and laughed the whole way across the Atlantic.

Back in NYC I settled down to enjoy my life of relaxation and luxury. Now that I was a married woman, surely I didn't need to work? Wrong! My husband was a hard taskmaster, and he immediately took me out to Central Park, where he gave me practice with my shorthand and told me to borrow a typewriter to improve my skills on that. I had three days, and then it was off to an agency.

I had left CC Company, as although I loved them all dearly, the work I had to do was really boring. However, I was somewhat nervous about trying to sell myself as a huge asset in any office. My dear friend Jean came to the rescue. Before she had returned to England, she gave me a small supply of lovely little yellow pills. Jean was a doctor's daughter, and she assured me they were safe and non-addictive. So before I went off to the employment agency for an interview, I took one of these tablets. I floated into the agency and assured them I was brilliant at shorthand and typing, and could speak three languages wonderfully well, and altogether, anybody would consider themselves incredibly lucky to be able to employ me.

I was sent to three job interviews. At the first one they almost went down on bended knee to employ me, and I told them I would let them know. At the second interview I was given a typing test. I could hardly read my shorthand back, but having a good short-term memory, I made up what I didn't know, and they were impressed, as I had used better English than they had! This time I was offered the job, more money and an office with my name on the door. I told them I would let them know.

At the employment agency I had taken advantage of being alone in the office for a while to peek at the job descriptions. The advertisement for the last job, at a wine importing firm had in large letters on the bottom of the page, 'MUST BE ATTRACTIVE!' I liked the sound of this one.

The brownstone building belonging to Frederick Wildman and Son off Madison Avenue was full of charm. I was interviewed by Mr Solon Kelly in a large room lined with bottles of wine, old pictures, lovely furniture and wonderful character. Solon was himself a very good-looking man. I sat demurely before him and crossed my legs, and begged him not to go too fast when he dictated. Bless him – he went so slowly I was able to take it all down in longhand! Solon offered me the job. I knew I wanted it, but I told him I would let him know, and wafted home.

Next morning the pill had worn off, and I was in a panic. I had been offered the most brilliant job, and I hadn't accepted it. I rang at once, and was told the job was mine, and I could start the next day.

Then reality hit me. I had fooled Solon with my languages – but in this job I would really need them. I was useless at shorthand and typing, and had never been a secretary in my life.

I took a pill on my first day. I serenely coped with everything I was asked to do, and even managed a bit of French translation. After a week of taking the pill, I spoke to myself most severely. I told myself the pill was not doing the work, I was – the pill only gave me confidence. Now I did not need it. I threw the rest of them away, and have never taken anything like them again in my life. They did a good job though!

Despite my lack of ability, the job was perfect for me, and I absolutely loved it. Solon took time to teach me about wine, and amazingly I muddled along. I was grateful to find that my desk was hidden around the corner from my boss, so he couldn't see me frantically looking up every word in the French dictionary.

"Take a letter, Elfrida, to be translated into French," he would say. "Yes, Mr Kelly" I would reply, and I would put on my best performance as the competent, linguistic secretary. Once typed up, the letter looked quite good. Solon would peruse it (he didn't speak French) and then say, "Very good Elfrida" while he signed it. The following week we would receive a wonderfully polite reply, so all was well – for the time being.

Our friends from the SS *Cristoforo Colombo* were still in NYC. We decided to have a reunion. After a splendid dinner, someone had the bright idea of going to a place called Sammy's Bowery Follies. By this time we were all extremely merry, so without a care in the world we took a taxi to downtown Manhattan and the Bowery.

Sammy's Bowery Follies was stuck in a time warp. It had been an old music hall theatre, but the auditorium was now filled with bare round tables and chairs. The stage was brightly lit, and two performers were dancing and singing in front of a painted backdrop of a chocolate box version of the countryside.

Once seated, I observed the performers. They both looked ancient – at least seventy years old. The lady was dressed in frills, picture-book hat and parasol, while the old man was in a striped blazer and boater. They were dire, but I always try to be kind to performers who are doing their best, so we cheered them on, and they obviously thought they were a great success.

The interval came, and Anne and I looked at each other and said, "We can do better than that". Before anyone could stop us, we were up on the stage and dancing the can-can to riotous enthusiasm from the audience, who sang along for us! I decided to make a spectacular finish, and leapt off the stage. I had no idea how high it was (very) or how hard the floor was (extremely), and I landed straight on my right knee. I felt nothing at all, but was surprised a few minutes later to discover my dress soaked in blood.

Next day I limped miserably into Wildman and Sons. Solon

told me, "We have an important visitor today Elfrida, the Italian vintner who produces the chianti we import."

"Yes Mr Kelly" I demurely replied, wondering if I was going to be asked to spout my limited Italian.

The visitor arrived and greeted Solon, who then called me to get some coffee. It was Renzo Olivieri.

"Elfie!" he cried, "how are you, and how is your knee?"

Solon looked from me to Renzo and said, "Do you two know each other then?" Once again he must have wondered what sort of 'secretary' he had hired.

One month later Richard and I went to a wonderful party. I still found it an incredibly heady experience being in a glamorous high-rise apartment overlooking the myriad lights of the Big Apple. I confess it all went to my head a bit, and I certainly didn't hold back in any way. At this particular party I met again a distant cousin of mine called Giles Gilbey, of the Gilbey gin family. We never knew each other well, but seeing each other in New York we decided we were the closest of relations, and needed to celebrate. This we did – big time!

Once again I dragged myself into work definitely the worse for wear. Solon was amused at my obvious extreme hangover. "Well you'll have to buck up" he said. "I have an important guest coming for a meeting."

Half an hour later the guest arrived. Yes, it was Giles Gilbey. Looking distinctly pale, he immediately asked Solon for black coffee. I was called to produce it. Neither Giles nor I said anything. Solon looked from him to me and back to Giles again, and then he said "Oh no! Don't tell me. You two know each other and were together last night?" We confessed, and Solon said to me, "Is there anyone in my business you don't know?"

After this I did settle down a bit, and continued with my

letters to Romanée Conti, Langenbach and Co., Ackerman et Laurence, Chapoutier and dear Renzo. The replies continued to come, and everyone thought I was doing very well. I was even asked to write descriptions about wines that were being used in our tasting events. My lack of knowledge was vast, but it didn't stop me being as inventive as possible. One line I was particularly proud of was "This wine cheerfully trickles down your throat, making you think of a little bubbling brook". I wonder if anyone bought this wine after reading that?

Wildman and Sons had been taken over by Almaden, the Californian wine growers. Great excitement was generated, as the first true champagne outside France, 'blanc de blancs' (made exclusively from the Chardonnay grape), had been produced after years of experimentation. We were chosen to hold the worldwide launch. Everyone who was anyone was invited, and the whole company was in a fever of excitement. Old Colonel Wildman himself was there, as was the CEO of Almaden. The speeches were made, and the bottles were lined up in inviting rows. With a huge flourish the first bottle was handed to Colonel Wildman.

He couldn't open it. He handed it to someone else. The second man couldn't do it either – in fact no one could open it, or any of the other bottles. One of my friends in the company begged me to help. I told him to break the bottle (out of sight) while I removed my stockings. We decanted the champagne through my stockings and declared to the guests that it was even better decanted. They appeared to agree, but our association with Almaden didn't last.

One day Solon gave me disconcerting news. The young son of our most important vintner in Bordeaux, Aubert de Villaine of Romanée Conti, was coming to New York to learn the

American side of his business. "The only problem" said Solon, "is that he can't speak English. Therefore I am giving you time off to show him around and translate for him."

I was sick with fear. I was about to be found out.

Aubert arrived in our office. He was tall, handsome and extremely charming. He tried a few words in halting English, but Solon immediately introduced me and explained I could speak French.

"Je m'excuse" I said, *"mais en verité je ne parle pas le Français. S'il vous plait, ne parles pas trop vite."*

Aubert looked at me for a while before shaking my hand and saying, *"Enchanté, Elfrida. Est ce que c'est possible que c'était vous qui a écrit les lettres?"*

"Oui" I murmured, and Aubert solemnly put his finger to his eye and said *"Mon oeil"* to indicate that my secret was safe with him.

Over the next few days Aubert and I did the rounds of New York City, and I introduced him to a friend of mine who was a guide at the UN and could speak French fluently. We had enormous fun, and Aubert took it upon himself to improve my French. He told me he and his family looked forward to my letters with joyous anticipation, as everyone gathered round and howled with laughter at my unbelievable French!

Aubert and I stayed in touch, and many years later Richard and I stayed with him and his American wife in Beaune, when Aubert still insisted on improving my French!

CHAPTER FIFTEEN

NEW YORK
AND LONDON

One beautiful Tuesday in late November 1963, I was allowed to leave the office early for an appointment. I happily strolled along Fifth Avenue to catch my bus uptown, glorying in the sunshine and sparkle of New York City. I saw two women standing still on the pavement. Something about their demeanour made me curious, and as I passed by I overheard one of them saying "Kennedy – and the Governor too."

While I was waiting at the bus stop I saw many people holding transistor radios to their ears, and when my bus came, the driver asked me what was going on out there. I told him what I had heard. During my walk back to my apartment I caught snatches of news from people's radios and televisions through open windows, and by the time I reached home I was convinced there had been an air crash.

The reality, as we all know, was a horror beyond belief. The entire country was engulfed in grief and shock. The young and charismatic President of the United States of America had been shot and killed in America, and worse than that, by a white American.

The next day the weather changed, and the sky deluged with rain which mingled with the tears and grief felt by everyone in the country. It was an extraordinary time to be in America.

President and Mrs Kennedy had been a breath of fresh air. Jacquie, glamorous and beautiful, and Jack with his good looks, together with their adorable young family, were totally different from any previous incumbents of the White House. The Kennedys became America's Royal Family, and Jacqueline was definitely the Princess.

I had been in New York during the Cuban Missile Crisis in October 1962. Russian war ships steamed towards Cuba, where aerial photography had discovered installations of missiles pointing at the United States. Jack Kennedy had given an address to the people on television and the nation had held its breath, as no one knew whether or not there would be a nuclear war within the next few hours. During these tense hours I was trying to concentrate on listening to Wagner's *Die Meistersinger* at the Metropolitan Opera House, but all I could do was wonder if I would be able to return to England.

Thankfully the Russian ships turned around at the last minute. You could almost hear the collective sigh of relief from the whole country.

Apart from such moments, Richard and I absolutely loved our time in New York. We were absurdly young and carefree, and had no responsibilities. We were so happy in our little apartment and decorated it with charm and originality. Richard's first attempt at putting up ready-pasted wallpaper was a bit of a disaster, as the whole lot came away in the night, and we had to fight our way through arches of wallpaper to reach the kitchen!

We found some great furniture, either at thrift (charity) shops, or left out on the street. Every week on a particular night people could leave out their unwanted furnishings, which were then collected the next day. Scavengers like us would wander round seeing what they could find. We found perfectly good carpets, two huge and comfortable armchairs and two charming corner cupboards. We also bought a chest of drawers known as a Low Boy, which still has pride of place in our house, and people assume came from my family! It was all such fun, and we were playing at being married.

We made some friends for life, and one of them, Buddy, (Baker Davis) later our son's godfather, owned a cabin in upstate New York at a place called Lost Lake. Lost Lake was pure magic. It was well named, as you couldn't tell it was there until you had driven through thick woodland, and there it was in all its tranquil beauty. From Buddy's cabin you were not aware of any other building, and it was the same for everyone. No motor boats were allowed, just canoes and rowing boats.

The cabin was simple in design. There was an outside 'long drop' and no hot water on tap. A wide deck fronted the lake, and under the trees Buddy had suspended the most comfortable Mexican marriage hammock. The other owners of cabins all became friends. They were actors, musicians and painters. We loved them all – and they loved us. We would have the most riotous evenings, which nearly always ended with someone making music while Buddy and I performed absurd dances together. Buddy was an artist and a dancer *manqué*.

We will never forget the enchanting people we met at Lost Lake, and feel privileged to have known them. The sight of Bill (a retired Shakespearean actor) and El, both in their seventies, coming to a party one evening dressed in their most absurd finery, with El sitting on a chair in their boat holding up a parasol while Bill rowed her across the lake, will stay with me forever. They are all gone from this earth now, but not from our hearts.

Richard and I were constantly amazed at how generous the Americans were towards us. Not only did Buddy become a godfather, but so did dear Eduardo Russell, husband of Carpy, who totally spoiled us with generosity, as did our lovely friend Dusty Weiss. How very lucky we were.

We were having dinner one night with a cousin of Dusty when he heard me saying how much I would love to visit Jamaica. "Oh I have a house there with a couple of servants doing nothing," he said. "I would be delighted if you would take it for your holiday."

I don't think we hesitated for a second. Jamaica was, we considered, our proper honeymoon. The house we were lent was old style, on the shores of the water near Montego Bay. We slept in a four-poster bed with mosquito nets, and the first night a rogue mosquito made its way inside the net. I chased it around with my slipper and as I swiped at it viciously, I fell down and the bed collapsed underneath me! We wondered what the manservant thought when he woke us up the next day.

In Jamaica I tasted my first mango. We met up with some people we knew, and after days of sun (larding ourselves with a good mixture of baby oil and iodine) and tennis, we would join up with our friends in the evening to sample the night life. We had rented a tiny convertible, and I did realize Richard was a little past driving one night when he complained the key wouldn't work as he tried to get into a Cadillac!

We had a picnic with our friends on Negril beach. Mateus Rosé was the wine of the moment and we did it proud. At that time of year it rained every afternoon at Negril. I found a suitable upturned canoe and joined by a scruffy stray dog, I slept my way through a violent thunderstorm that lasted an hour. We then swam out a very long way to the coral reef. Not being a very good swimmer I decided to return to the beach, as I had also scratched myself quite badly on the coral. I was accompanied the whole way by a small fish that swam under my stomach. I couldn't get rid of it – and it looked remarkably like a small shark. I was not far wrong, as I later discovered. This fish was a pilot fish, and pilot fish swim ahead of sharks to find them tasty meals. Glad I didn't know that at the time!

We made the most of our time in the Big Apple, and enjoyed the glamour of life in the Hamptons during the summer months while relishing the Fall Foliage during the autumn. Winter found us attempting to ski, although I was useless, as my ballet training would not allow me to bend forward, and I found keeping my knees parallel hard, as they automatically wanted to turn out. Not very helpful when learning to ski!

New York positively glistens at Christmas time. One morning, after the hugest blizzard, we all awoke with a start to find the great city completely silent and cloaked in pristine white. And during a gale once, Richard and I had to hold on to each other as we tried to cross a road, with debris flying everywhere. We loved it all, the sounds, the sights and the smells that combined to produce the New York City of the sixties.

Dear Lost Lake friends gave a party in their huge apartment on the West Side of Manhattan overlooking the Hudson River. Our host was an accomplished drummer, and when another guest started to play the piano it was only natural that Buddy and I would dance.

As we were leaving, the piano-playing guest, Bill, suggested we shared a cab back to the East Side. He then invited us to his apartment for a nightcap. Having to work the next day did not deter us and we happily agreed.

Somewhat to our surprise, the taxi came to a halt outside an office building, as opposed to an apartment block. Our new friend simply said "Follow me". Then he opened a door and led us across an empty lobby to a vast lift. Up we went to the top floor, and I recall seeing a huge room full of desks in serried ranks, each with a covered typewriter on top quietly resting for the night.

Slightly nervous, we continued to follow Bill through a door which led outside to fire escape steps which we climbed, finally coming to a large door at the end of a parapet. When this door was opened we gasped in amazement. We had been transported into the most wonderful apartment, with staggering views on three sides and a huge fireplace on the fourth wall. It was beautifully furnished with bookshelves from floor to ceiling. On a raised dais in between two full-length windows stood a grand piano.

"I own the building" Bill explained. "This way I can play the piano at all hours of the day or night and not disturb anyone."

Richard and I stayed until the small hours of the morning, singing, dancing and listening to Bill's music. He was to become a great friend and another unique individual who helped enrich our early life together in New York City.

Richard had persuaded his sister Julie to join us while we were living in New York. Julie became a very successful literary agent, with many famous clients, and she remained living in this city for the rest of her working life. She did have a bit of a problem once when she tried to tell a telephone operator she wanted a book sent to 'Rose Cottage.' No way could the operator understand 'cottage'. Julie resorted to almost screaming as she said "cottage – a SMALL HOUSE." Finally the operator understood. "Oh you mean CARDEDGE!" Julie then understood the meaning of "divided by a common language"!

Despite our happiness, we reluctantly decided it was time to return to England. We had so many friends from different walks of life, and had experienced extraordinary times. Because we were young and English, and also probably quite jolly, we were seemingly fairly popular, so we were very spoilt. It was a precious time in our lives, and we knew it could never be repeated. The decision was made, and my husband was able to transfer to the London office of Young and Rubicam.

I hated having to tell Wildman and Sons I was leaving. Solon gave me a delightful farewell present of the silver regalia of the Chevalier du Tastevin (which of course I had not earned). This gift meant so much to me, but a year later it was among many items we lost in a burglary, and the year after that dear Solon died of cancer.

After several more farewell parties and many tears, we found ourselves on board my darling ship, the RMS *Queen Elizabeth*. Richard and I stood on the deck, and both of us had tears pouring down our faces as we pulled away from the dock, sailed under the Verrazano Narrows Bridge and left behind our family, our friends and the first years of our married life.

★ ★ ★

BUMP! We were back in London before we knew it, and it did not take long for the realisation to sink in that the carefree start to our married life was well and truly over.

We lived at home in Victoria Road while we looked for a house. My other aunt, Meme, lived there as well and ran the house. Each day she asked us if we would be in for the evening meal. If we changed our minds at all, she let her annoyance show clearly. It was horrible not being our own masters any more. I now joyfully discovered that I was pregnant, but I began to feel rather unwell as a result, and this did not help.

My mother was volatile, and it seemed hard to please her. I was endlessly doing the wrong thing. Richard's new job took him away for a night a week, and often he didn't leave the office until terribly late, which ruined dinner and made us even more unpopular. We weren't used to this - we were used to adoration! Oh dear – why had we come home?

Luckily we found a house in Northumberland Place, north London, a charming Georgian terrace house with a wrought-iron balcony. I couldn't wait to move in.

Mummy helped me with decoration. She had a great flair for doing houses. The only problem was that I was never allowed an opinion. She also loved to shop without me, and then present me with her purchases. One dreadful day I said, "I wish you would let me come with you so we can choose together." My poor Mama completely lost her cool, and accused me of being totally ungrateful. She then said she would do nothing more and swept out of the house. Richard came home to find me awash with tears, but even he couldn't persuade my mother to talk to me.

We finished the house, and we decided Mummy and Meme would be our first guests in our dining room. Poor Richard – when I married him I could only cook the one meal that Filly had taught me, Wiener Schnitzel and cucumber salad. Our dinner parties in New York only survived my dreadful cooking because at Wildman I had had to test each shipment of wine for their alcoholic content. This required taking the tiniest bit of wine from a bottle of each vintage. I had therefore planned my dinner parties around this job, and would stagger home with one bottle each of terrific wines such as La Tâche, Romanée Conti, Puligny Montrachet and the best that Louis Latour and Chapoutier could offer. Everyone loved our dinner parties!

On the occasion of my dinner for my mother, I decided to make a quiche Lorraine. It was a near disaster, saved by Meme, but my naughty mother still refused to talk to me, and sat through the entire dinner reading magazines. I like to think that now my husband would have said something, but at just twenty-eight, and not having a mother of his own, he felt he couldn't. My baby was very nearly due, and I was distraught.

Mummy had insisted I went to the Queen's gynaecologist, despite the fact he had retired from 'babies'. Mr J decided I was late, and should be taken into hospital and induced. I didn't think I was late, but did as I was told.

In hospital my waters were broken and I was given drugs to induce contractions. After several hours it was agreed that the baby was not going to come, so Richard was told to go home and I was given two huge sleeping tablets. I was in a little room adjoining the main ward at the Middlesex Hospital. I begged R to stay until I was asleep. Although I drifted in and out of sleep I was continuously awoken by very strong contractions. Richard would wake up and rub my back as he had been taught, with vim, vigour and determination. This went on all night. No one looked in on me and my young husband didn't think to ring the bell or find a nurse.

Morning came and we could hear all the squalling babies being taken to their mothers for food. We kept quiet and waited patiently. The door then opened and the night nurse couldn't believe Richard was still there. The baby's heartbeat was checked, and then, as they say, "all hell broke loose".

I was so out of it I hardly knew what was going on. Mr J had been woken from his slumbers and politely asked me if I would agree to a caesarean. No sooner had I acquiesced than the door was open and I was being rushed to the operating theatre at top speed.

I remember nothing more until I awoke in a large private room and from somewhere above me Richard's head swam into view and told me we had a son. At the farthest end of the room was the disembodied figure of my mother, who wouldn't come anywhere near me. Little did we know what was happening to my mother, but the hurt I felt was tangible, and what with the shock of the whole birth, and my very sore tummy, I was annoyingly sad, despite being thrilled to be the mother of an enchanting baby boy.

Baby Tim and I had only been home a day when I begged Richard to ring Mummy to invite her over. He was ages on the telephone, and when he finally appeared, his face was very grim. He told me that Mummy had had a massive stroke and was unconscious and partly paralysed.

It was too much to take in all at once. As soon as I could, I went to see her in her pretty bedroom in Victoria Road. Mummy was awake, but she couldn't speak. She could only grunt. A few days later she began to speak, but only in German, her first language. The next stage was speaking in English, but rubbish. She could not find the right words, and became furious with us if we didn't understand her.

Tim was born on 23rd June 1965. It was a hot summer, and soon we all went to Fritham and there with the help of my sisters and my aunts I finally began to relax and enjoy my baby, and Mummy gradually improved.

My mother was brilliant in the way she coped with the aftermath of her stroke. She never regained the use of her right side, but my goodness she tried. She did however regain her speech, and her wonderful sense of humour. Years later she used to love me telling her what she had been like initially, and I had to act it out in great detail. She would roar with laughter. Mummy taught herself not only to write again, in a clear round style, but to paint with her left hand. As soon as she could, she would take herself off to Harrods to shop!

Richard and I began to settle into London life. Our immediate neighbour was Justin de Blanc. Justin, originally an advertising man, was a serious foodie. He later opened a chain of extremely successful delicatessen-style shops in London. Richard still went away every week, so with his permission, Justin would borrow me for his dinner parties to act as his hostess. The baby alarm was somehow connected to his house with long wires. At these parties I met the most fascinating people, including many famous writers and artists of the day.

Baby number two was now on the way, and we decided we needed to move. We found a house in Lansdowne Road W11, although we did not appreciate what a brilliant buy this was. The house needed a great deal doing to it, and the builders were still there when I went into hospital. Again I went to the Middlesex, although not Mr J this time. Young Nicholas John was also born by caesarean, but all went well. Annoyingly, however, a new theatre was being constructed on the floor above me, and the noise was so horrendous that R had to buy me some earplugs. I hated putting the baby to sleep in the nursery with this racket going on overhead. In those days one had to stay for two weeks in hospital after a caesarean birth. It was not much quieter at home, so I escaped to the calm of the New Forest.

A few months later I began to suspect that Nicholas could not hear very well. Richard and I tested him at home, and he had to agree with me. We went to our GP, who dropped metal instruments onto a metal tray, and the baby didn't even blink.

An appointment was arranged with a top Harley Street specialist. Richard came from work and we went in together. The verdict from this eminent man was that Nick was totally and completely deaf, and the sooner we learned sign language the better. He did say though that we should go to the audiology department at Great Ormond Street to assess the degree of deafness.

During the weeks while we waited for the appointment, I found out all I could about deaf children and their education. I looked at my lovely little baby, and tried to visualise what his life would be like not hearing a voice, a bird sing, the sound of the sea or music. My heart was breaking with sadness for him – and for us.

We sat nervously in the waiting room at the famous children's hospital, and anticipated the complicated tests Nick would undoubtedly have to suffer. It was therefore with a great deal of scepticism that I sat with Nicholas (then aged about nine months) on my lap on one side of a small wooden table, with a doctor on the other. This man picked up a dinky toy car and dropped it on the table.

"Well" he said, "he is not totally deaf." We said nothing. Next a large and very noisy squeaky doll was produced and the doctor squeezed it behind Nick's right ear. No response. Same with the left, and the same non-reaction when he squeaked it above and behind his head. Richard and I looked at each other miserably.

The doctor then gave Nick the doll to hold and play with for a bit. He squeezed it a few times. He then repeated the movements he had done earlier, and Nick followed every one. The specialist repeated this exercise with ever-decreasing sounds, until he was rubbing two sponges together. Once he knew what was making the sound, Nick looked for it.

"Has this baby been subjected to a lot of noise in his short life?" we were asked. On hearing our reply, he assured us there was nothing the matter at all with Nick's hearing, it was just that he had mastered the ability to 'switch off' any sound that didn't interest him. He noted my disbelief, and made an appointment for six months hence, which he assured me I would not need to keep. He was correct!

★ ★ ★

Lansdowne Road was a fabulous house for us. It was a large terrace which backed onto a vast communal garden.

We instantly made friends with our neighbours, and the boys, as they grew older, had the most enormous fun with the other children in the beautiful garden. At one stage I even became Chairman of the Garden Committee.

Shortly before Nicholas had been born, I had been approached by my old ballet teacher, Enid Murray, to see if I would be interested in taking over the teaching of ballet at Lady Eden's School. Would I! It would be like coming home, and I was absolutely thrilled. Enid taught all the ballet classes, while Miss Betty Vacani taught the kindergarten children.

For five very happy years I was the Ballet Mistress at Lady Eden's School. Amongst my pupils was Mary Bethune's little girl, Lucy. It was apparent from the start that Lucy had great talent, and eventually she was accepted at the Royal Ballet School before becoming a very successful soloist in the Rambert Ballet Company. Incidentally, she also, in years to come, became my daughter's godmother.

The Headmistress in those days was Mrs Helen Wakeford. She was another inspirational and gifted teacher, and she became a very close friend.

Not being able to afford a trained nanny, we would hire young girls who wanted to work with children and dress them up in nanny uniforms. On the whole we were extremely lucky and had some wonderful girls. There were also some disasters, and combined with the collection of 'au pair' girls we had, I could seriously write a whole book about them and nothing else!

One dreadful day I was teaching at the school when Helen entered the hall and told me to go home at once, as the nanny had let Tim (aged three) out in the garden on his own, and hadn't checked on him for ages. Then she had discovered that the gate to Holland Park Avenue had been left open by some workmen, and Tim had disappeared.

During the drive home I did my best to keep calm, but I was feeling sick with fear. There was still no sign of Tim when I reached the house, but the police told me to stay put in case he was found. All I wanted to do was to rush out and look for him. My biggest worry was that he had been kidnapped.

Mercifully, we did not have too long to wait. Someone was definitely watching over my little boy that day, as all by himself he had crossed the busy Holland Park Avenue and somehow made his way to the Portobello Road. There he was spotted by a woman who rightly guessed he was lost, and took him to Holland Park Police Station.

I was so unbelievably grateful to have my child back unharmed that I was not cross with the nanny, as she had had the most dreadful shock herself and learned her lesson as well.

Socially life was a whirl. We often gave parties where Richard would mix the most lethal champagne cocktails. "I want to make sure everybody has a good time" he would say. They did!

This was London in the swinging sixties - Carnaby Street, Biba, Mary Quant, mini-skirts, Twiggy and the musical *Hair*. The city was on fire! All of a sudden we felt free to experiment with clothes, hair - and drugs. The Teddy Boys were a laugh, but they were another way of breaking out of the dreary post-war mould. The 'Flower Power' of San Francisco and the influence of songs from America encouraged the use of psychedelic drugs amongst people of all ages, from every walk of life.

I grew my hair and wore the shortest skirts, teamed with tight white or shiny black knee-length boots. I may have been a mother of two and a dedicated ballet teacher, but I was still only twenty-seven and I was ready to 'rock 'n' roll'.

During this time we met someone who was to become a lifelong friend, the broadcaster David Jacobs. Through David we met people from the world of show business as well as modelling. Pauline Stone and Lawrence Harvey eventually shared a nanny with us. Dorothy Bond and Sandra Paul were both stunningly beautiful, and Sandra married our close friend Nigel Grandfield before eventually marrying Michael Howard, who later became Leader of the Conservative Party. After ending her modelling career, Sandra turned to writing, and is now a successful novelist.

Derek Nimmo and his charming wife Pat became good friends. Patrick Lichfield, the Queen's cousin and famous photographer, came to our parties, but sadly I was never photographed by him.

I was lucky enough to be photographed by several famous photographers. The first was known as Baron, and he was the last word in brilliance. He was very well known for his fabulous ballet photographs, but I posed for him as a child, and the results were charming. The wonderful Barry Swaebe and his sister Betty, Tom Hustler and Walter Bird, along with the brilliant Inge Morath, who eventually married Arthur Miller, were all kind enough to photograph me at different stages of my life.

Richard and I did not dabble in drugs. We didn't need to - the life we were leading was heady enough, and we went to so many glamorous events and exciting new night clubs that any more thrills would have been *de trop*!

By this time we were members of Annabel's, the famous club in Berkeley Square, and on one occasion I relinquished my seat for two guests who had nowhere to go; they were Princess Margaret and Peter Sellers.

Apart from Tim and Nick, we had three other important members of our family. Babar was our very large and boisterous chocolate brown giant poodle. Even sitting down, he was taller than three-year-old Nick. Babar was a fabulous dog and highly intelligent. His two companions were black and white cats called Salome and Fred. Fred had been called Celeste until we realised his sex. When we gave Babar a last walk at night, Fred would accompany us but kept to the gardens in front of the houses.

CHAPTER SIXTEEN

THE OTHER SIDE OF
THE WORLD: 1972-1977

Everything was going so well, and we were really enjoying our life in London. So why did we decide, when the boys were just five and seven years old, to leave it all behind and go to Australia to live? The opportunity just presented itself.

Richard was moving with the company he then worked for, McCann Erickson, and they decided we should emigrate, for £10 each and £5 for the boys! We had to undertake not to return to the UK for two years. In return for this the company paid for a rented house for us in Sydney for six months.

It was desperately hard to leave my family, especially my mother. I hated relinquishing my job, and leaving our friends made us miserable. I refused to sell our beautiful house, so we let it through a friend, to the American Embassy.

We both began to have the most dreadful cold feet, and wondered what on earth we were doing. We had so many emotional farewell parties, and there was the agony of parting with our beloved animals as well as my family and dearest friends. I was torn in two, and terrified we were making the most ghastly mistake. When we finally boarded the plane I was so exhausted that I slept practically the whole way, which in those days took 32 hours with five stops en route.

I wondered if I would see my mother again, and my heart felt very sad.

* * *

"Welcome to the land of the Lolly Gobble Bliss Bombs!"

Never will we forget the unusual words which greeted us as we stumbled off the plane after a seemingly endless journey. Nick, who hadn't slept the entire way from London to Australia, decided to curl up on the floor and lapse into the deepest sleep just as we were making our preparations to land.

Those unexpected words of welcome were uttered by one of Richard's new colleagues, and he followed them up by presenting the boys with a package of the aforementioned Bliss Bombs, which were in fact candied popcorn. This kind man was so keen to show us the sights that he gave us a quick guided tour of Sydney before driving us into the suburb of French's Forest to find our house. Regrettably we were all in such a zombie-like state that not much filtered into our brains!

The house was fine, and completely different from anything we had ever lived in. It was in a quiet cul de sac and stood high up the hill on the left, while on the other side of the road the houses sloped down the hill.

It was a beautiful winter's day in July. The blue skies and bright sun which caught the wings of the galahs and other parakeets flying overhead added to our feeling of excitement and anticipation about our new life ahead. Nick did not quite understand the distance we had travelled, and asked to go to see Granny the following weekend.

Richard was given a company car, an aubergine-coloured Charger. He realised I had to have a car as well, so he bought me an extremely old, but full of character, VW Beetle. When he left every day to drive to the office on the other side of the Harbour Bridge, the boys and I explored.

If truth be told, this was a truly magical time with my two little boys. I had been so frantic in the lead up to our departure from England that they had by necessity been rather neglected. I had not kept my promise to tell them my invented stories of Rajah the White Elephant on the journey, as they constantly reminded me.

For two months I gave them school lessons every morning, while we spent the afternoons discovering the fantastic beaches and fascinating national parks in the area. Unfortunately I did end up in a ditch one day, as I had forgotten that the car was heavier at the back because of the position of the engine. We were rescued by a Crocodile Dundee character who refused any reward for his kind help, as hearing our accents was enough!

When the school holidays started the boys began to make friends with the neighbouring children. I made friends as well, although I knew we were not going to stay in French's Forest. We had decided to buy a house in the Eastern Suburbs, and consequently enrolled the boys in a school called Cranbrook.

I didn't like to leave the children with a sitter, but one day I was told I really must so I could attend an office lunch party. I hired a respectable-looking woman from an agency, and rang her before we left to return home, to ensure all was well. It was, then, but when we arrived back, the house was full of children, except that there was no sign of Tim or Nick. Unfortunately Nicholas had ridden his little bike very fast down the steep slope on the right side of the road, and crashed straight into a garage wall. The kindly neighbours had driven him miles to hospital, taking Tim with them to keep him company. He survived – with six stitches to his head.

Because we had not sold our house in London, we had less to play with, and found ourselves unable to buy the sort of house we had dreamed about. We ended up in a house not unlike Northumberland Place. It was a charming terraced house in the area of Sydney known as Paddington, and it too had a wrought iron balcony.

When the boys started at Cranbrook my life was not quite so much fun, as we were still north of the harbour. We had to leave our house very early each day, and as I had to pick up Nick before Tim it was not worth my while to return to French's Forest. I had nowhere to go, and would often just sit in my little car somewhere and write letters home. Life improved when we moved into Hargrave Street, but I still felt extremely homesick, and missed my London life.

I found our first Christmas incredibly hard. The weather was unbelievably hot. We decided to give Tim a bike, but it came in parts, and do-it-yourself is not Richard's forte. He struggled in the heat on the balcony, and it did look like a bicycle on Christmas Day, but didn't survive a test ride!

I found an evergreen branch to substitute for a Christmas

tree and after a semi-festive lunch we went to Bondi Beach for a swim. It did not feel at all like Christmas, and my mind wandered back in time to those early Christmas days when my father had been alive.

The boys settled into their new schools very quickly and began to make friends. I realised I had to make a bit of effort and stop feeling sorry for myself. I made myself talk to the mothers of the boys' school friends, and in no time made some wonderful new friends who I have kept to this day.

Before long we found ourselves swept up in the fun and joy of living in Sydney in the 1970s. Richard was enjoying his job, and he had a fabulous office overlooking the iconic Sydney Opera House and the ever-busy harbour.

The boys loved their new school, and rapidly picked up Australian accents. Nicholas did disgrace himself once, as he and his friend James Paker decided it would be fun to 'streak' across the playing field when a match was in progress. Both boys were six years old, and both mothers found it hard to keep a straight face as we were severely reprimanded by the Headmistress and our sons were duly punished.

As soon as I stopped being silly and hiding myself away, I found people to be more than welcoming. Parties were given, and we were introduced to many traditional Sydney pastimes, my favourite being eating fresh prawns on Bondi beach on a Sunday morning.

Amongst our friends were Carrie and Peter Vickers, who had two children called Jossie and Willy. Jossie was a stunningly beautiful child. Her white blonde hair fell half way down her back, framing an enchanting heart-shaped face, with a dear little mouth. In the summer she was the perfect mermaid, diving into the water with her hair contrasting with her glistening, tanned little body.

Jossie was completely unaware of how beautiful she was or the effect she had on other people. She had a strong character, and felt deeply about certain issues, especially anything to do with cruelty to animals. But tragedy was lurking. All her life, Jossie had suffered from extreme bouts of asthma, and had been close to death on numerous occasions. Nothing slowed her up however, and her strong opinions often brought her into conflict with the other children. Her mother, Carrie, used to say to me "Elfie, you and Jossie are both Geminis, and you are the only person she will listen to – please will you do something about her?" There was no doubt about it, Jossie and I got on extremely well, and I thought she was the most unusual and gorgeous child I had ever met.

One day Richard said to me, "Do you think we should try for another baby?" My reply was – "If you can guarantee we will have a little girl like Jossie, I would be delighted."

We didn't have long to wait before a new baby was on the way, and Jossie knew that I was hoping for a little girl just like her. When Laura was born in March 1974 Jossie was so very excited, and told everyone that Laura was indeed her very special baby.

The dreadful day I answered the telephone a few months later will stay with me forever. Another friend was trying desperately to tell me through her tears that Jossie had suffered a very severe asthma attack, and that by the time she had arrived at hospital, her heart had stopped, and that beautiful, enchanting little girl had died. If ever there was a candidate for an angel in heaven, Jossie was a certainty.

Amid the tragedy, Richard and I could not believe that we now had our own little girl to complete our family. I had visions of at last being able to indulge in beribboned hair and pretty little dresses. Alas, my dear daughter wanted to be just like her big brothers. She refused to wear any girly clothes, and told everyone that she was in fact a boy! At this stage her brothers were nine and seven years old.

We made some new friends called John and Maggie Cooper. They had two little girls who had attended Lady Eden's School when they had lived in London. Years later we are now neighbours in Wiltshire. A big hop from Bondi to Devizes!

One year we decided to return to New York via California in order to meet my wonderful cousin Richard Gully, whom I mentioned earlier. We had a fantastic time at the film studios, and then RG gave a dinner party for us at a restaurant called Le Bistro, which we were assured was THE best restaurant in Hollywood. We also sat at THE best table. How delighted RG was when Peter Sellers came in with his friends and was unable to get our table. That was the second time we had been competing with Peter for the same space!

I sat next to Glenn Ford, and my husband was next to Merle Oberon. Merle later came to Sydney, when we saw her again. She was part American Indian and stunningly beautiful.

After our dinner we went to George Hamilton's house for a party. It was good to see George again, by this time married to Alana. Everything in the house was in black and white, including a black man dressed in a white suit playing a black piano on a white carpet. I was having a whale of a time meeting actors whose names were so familiar to me, like Zsa Zsa Gabor, Robert Stack and Vincente Minelli. My poor husband was continually being given the cold shoulder, until it was explained that he was an advertising man living in Australia and not an up-and-coming actor. Thanks to his good looks, the male actors were jealous of him!

Two years later 1 was in California again, this time on my own. A dear friend of my cousin, Francie Whittenberg, hosted an amazing party for me. This was in the private room at Le Bistro, and about 50 people attended for dinner. There was an orchestra playing, and a young man sang a song especially for me. My dinner companion was Charlton Heston, and Cyd Charisse was also at my table. Everybody there was either a well-known performer or director. A speech was given to welcome me to Hollywood.

I was so excited to meet Charlton Heston at the party. He was another great star, and I adored him in *Chariots of Fire*. I was somewhat disappointed to see how small he was, but assumed it was my fault being so tall. He was very charming to me and we had great fun talking about a variety of subjects.

The whole evening was quite surreal, as nobody had the faintest idea who I was or why I was there. The fact that Richard had invited them was enough, as they hoped he would write about them in his column.

After the song and the speech I felt I had to say something, so I hope I gave one of my better performances when I stood up and thanked everyone for their wonderful kindness in welcoming me to Hollywood. With a tear in my eye I assured them that I would never forget such a wonderful evening. I had a huge round of applause, and then with one accord, everybody rose to their feet, said their goodbyes and left. I was driven all by myself to the palatial mansion 1 had been lent, and it was only 10.30pm.

I was delighted that I eventually managed to persuade Richard Gully to return to England for the first time since he had left as a young man. In some small way I was able to repay him for the years of enjoyment he had given to me and our friends, including David and Lindsay Jacobs, Derek and Pat Nimmo and Michael and Sandra Howard. They all greatly enjoyed meeting him and hearing his wonderful stories when they dined with us.

It was during a subsequent party held for Richard Gully that I had my second encounter with James Bond, although this time it was not Sean Connery. Among the guests were Roger Moore and his attractive wife Kristina Tholstrup. Sandra Howard, who was there with her husband Michael, and I gazed with envy, awe and wonderment at the sight of Kristina's pearls. Without doubt they were the longest and most beautiful rope of pearls either of us had ever seen.

I was duly introduced to my second 007, and as I gazed into that famous face, I put on a look of puzzled bewilderment as I said, "I am so sorry, I am afraid I don't know who you are." Being the charming man he is, Roger immediately replied, "Oh forgive me. My name is Roger Moore".

I then confessed. "Of course I know who you are really" I said, "I just thought it would be a novelty for you not to be recognised!"

I am happy to recall that Roger saw the funny side, and we continued to have a long and enjoyable conversation, mostly about my dear cousin.

★ ★ ★

Soon after Laura's birth, plans were made for my mother to come and stay with us in Australia. Despite being semi-paralysed after her stroke, Mummy was still able to get herself about, and she decided to come to Australia via New York, where she stayed with my aunt Phil, and then Jamaica, where my sister Rose was living at the time.

As soon as Mummy arrived in Sydney, she declared that we must leave our house in Hargrave Street and move to a bigger and lighter house. She and I then started house hunting, and together we found a modern, but definitely light and airy house in Dover Heights, complete with swimming pool, which the boys thought was heaven. It also had a view of the harbour, which we loved.

Before we moved in, however, Mummy insisted I took her shopping to a department store called Grace Bros. I was not yet fully recovered from my third caesarean and would have preferred not to, but she insisted. We parked in the multi-storey car park, and I struggled to heave the cumbersome pram out of the back seat and attach it to the wheels. As Mummy couldn't manage steps, we started to walk slowly down the ramps trying to avoid the cars as they came up.

Suddenly, to my horror, just as a car was approaching, the entire top of the pram rolled off its base and my darling baby was thrown out onto the concrete ramp. The first thing my mother said was, "It's all right, she didn't hit her head". She was right, and although Laura had a very nasty bump, she was not, in fact injured. I was shocked beyond reason, and all I wanted to do was to go home. Was I allowed to? Certainly not! We were in the shop now, so there we were going to stay. The baby looked deathly pale, and I kept on poking her. But she survived, as did I, and Mummy enjoyed her shopping.

We moved into our new house, and at once Mummy proved herself to be the most amazing babysitter, despite only having the use of one arm. She scooped Laura up by grabbing the back of her clothes, and she was able to do everything for her except fasten the safety pin on her nappy. No disposables then. Added to this, my mother made friends of her own. Everybody adored her, and she was in her element recounting various stories of her life.

After six months my mother decided it was time to return to England. We were all sad, as the visit had turned out to be the greatest success, and she adored Sydney, saying it reminded her of Canada. Once home, she wrote to me saying that the past six months had been the happiest of her life. The little boys had also enjoyed seeing so much of their Granny, and she was so unpressured in her life with us that she had time to play games with them and read stories. I treasure the memories of those months, and am just so happy I was in a position to give her such a happy time.

Mrs Woods, aka Woody, then came into our lives. Laura adored her, and whenever there was the need, Laura would go and live with Woody, in the next door street.

We had decided to take the boys on an adventurous holiday to the Far East, and this meant leaving my jolly little baby behind. I knew Woody would take the greatest care of her – but I hated saying goodbye.

We planned our holiday meticulously through our friendly travel agent in Sydney. We were all extremely excited, as this was to be our first experience in the Far East.

Singapore was our first stop, staying at the Shangri-La Hotel. We were initially bowled over by the heat, and wilted somewhat as we were whisked round the sights every tourist should see. We visited the Tiger Balm Gardens and the Jade House, as well as the Botanic Gardens and Boat Quay. It was with a sense of relief that we returned to the hotel to relax by the outdoor swimming pool before we embarked on the evening's activities.

Richard was larking about in the pool, as was his wont, with the boys. I was stretched out on a sun lounger, practically asleep.

Suddenly I heard my husband's strangled voice say "Darling!" and I looked up to see him leaning over the edge of the pool with blood pouring down his face. I leapt up and rushed over to him in a state of anxiety and shock, and as I bent over to see how badly he was hurt, I promptly fainted!

Of course, I never lived it down. There he was, injured and bloody, and there was I, prone on the deck and two little boys still in the pool in a somewhat concerned state!

He was fine – after a butterfly stitch or two – and the mishap luckily did not impede our evening plans. We ate in the 'car park restaurant' – quite delicious - and then wandered about enjoying the atmosphere. Just before midnight we left the boys asleep in the hotel room. We had told them we were going out, but of course we had no mobile phones then, so they had no way of contacting us. However, cruel and thoughtless parents that we were, we were determined to go to Bugis Street.

Bugis Street was famous in those days for the sight of beautiful and sexy women parading themselves in all their fashionable glory. The only drawback was that none of them were in fact women - they were all young men. I found it quite fascinating, and try as I might, I could not tell they were male. Richard was the recipient of many a good-natured invitation, but I was ignored. We sat and had a drink - and then a flock, a shoal of sailors arrived. They were Australian, and had been at sea for at least four months, and they were 'ready to go'!

Their chief asked if he could join our table. He then told us that if any of his sailors were silly enough to accept what these 'girls' offered, they would wake up several hours later with a very sore head and no wallet! He had warned them, but they wouldn't listen. This man then turned to me and said, "What a relief it is for me to be sitting here and talking to a beaut little

Ozzie redhead sheila like yourself." I knew then that I had arrived!

We had a friend who had invited us to stay with her and her husband in Borneo. Toots and Moray Watson, with their baby, lived on a remote oil palm plantation in Sabah. The only way to reach their house was by the air or the river. Moray took my three fellows to Mount Kinabalu. After their first night spent on the mountain Tim felt sick, and had to be taken down again. Nick continued with his father and the guide, and reached the highest guest house before he too succumbed to exhaustion.

My fury knew no bounds when I heard that my husband had been so determined to reach the peak that he had left our little nine-year-old on his own in the hut for hours. They both survived unharmed, thankfully, or my husband's life would not have been worth living! The boys were fascinated by the whole experience, especially meeting a member of the last surviving tribe of head hunters.

Our next stop was Kuala Lumpur, followed by Bangkok, where we stayed in the magnificent Oriental Hotel. Never had we experienced such incredible service. We slept in bedrooms with silk-covered walls and sat gazing out of the windows at the busy life on the river, while tasting an abundance of strange tropical fruit, the like of which we had never seen before, star fruit, rambutans, pomelos and so on.

Nicholas's tastes were quite conservative, and hamburgers and spaghetti Bolognese were all he wanted to eat. Tim was more grown-up, and sat with us in the restaurant on the top of the Oriental bravely trying new and exotic dishes while Nick stayed by himself in the coffee shop in the basement.

We thought Bangkok was so exciting. We eventually came to know the Grand Temple and the Floating Market, along with other sights, very well, but on this occasion we looked and savoured with awe. We visited the House on the Klong where the American Jim Thompson, who had founded the Thai silk industry in Bangkok, used to live. It was a treasure trove of beautiful objects, and was cared for by the American Women's League. Jim Thompson himself disappeared in the Cameron Highlands one day. It was rumoured he was working for the CIA, but nobody knows for sure what happened to him.

From Bangkok we flew up to Chiang Mai, which forms part of the Golden Triangle with Burma and India and is an area known for growing opium poppies. We stayed in a charming hotel right in the centre, and during the day we visited the hill tribes. We had to negotiate incredibly rough roads which were hair-raising to say the least, as we noticed upturned vehicles half way down the mountain. We had chains on our wheels to try to prevent us following suit.

The first tribe, called the Meo, all wore black. The women wore the most intricately-embroidered concertina-pleated heavy skirts, while the children wore enchanting caps embroidered and decorated with silver. The women did all the work in the village. They took a year to make a skirt, and changed it when the new one was finished. Babies under a year old were not allowed to touch the ground, so children as young as three and four had to carry their little siblings round with them. The men sat inside their huts smoking opium. Neither Richard nor I had seen a village like this before, and our boys were completely fascinated and full of questions.

The next day we visited the White Karen hill tribe. As expected they all wore white, often decorated with coloured ribbons and silver. I found it somewhat horrific to see the little girls covered in western make-up which had been given to them by tourists, and nearly all of them were smoking cheroots.

Back in our hotel we had noticed a family that we couldn't quite make out. They struck us as rather elderly to have the small child who was with them, and yet not old enough to be its grandparents. On our last night we decided to eat somewhere different, and when we arrived, only one table was left – right next door to these people. We had a drink together afterwards, and they said, "Please forgive us, but we have been trying to work you out. You two are obviously English, and yet somehow you have managed to adopt two little Australian boys who look so much like you. How did that come about?" We all had a good laugh about that. We discovered that they were indeed the parents of the small child, and had an even younger one back home.

From Chiang Mai we flew to Penang, where we stayed in an enormous hotel called the Rasa Sayang. This was obviously a very popular place for expat families to stay, and when I saw all the toddlers careering about and having a wonderful time I found myself missing my little girl very much.

The Snake Temple was the high point as far as the boys were concerned. This was a small temple absolutely teeming with somnolent, sedated snakes of every description. The incense kept them in this state, and there was a horrid fascination in watching them.

The following day we rented a car, and braved the ghastly and dangerous roads to drive to Ipoh. We were so looking forward to discovering remnants of the Colonial past in the shape of the magnificent railway station, and especially our hotel, the Lake View Hotel. But Ipoh was a huge shock. It was filthy and crowded. The street market we passed looked an open invitation to all sorts of diseases, as the drains were totally choked with muck, debris and rats.

At last we arrived at our hotel. But what was this? No sumptuous lobby opened before our eyes, and no uniformed flunkeys came rushing out to grab our bags and offer us cooling drinks. Instead there was a tiny entrance with one man behind a glass-fronted case. This case displayed all the paraphernalia one would need for an overnight stay, razors, toothbrushes, tiny bars of soap etc.

Richard and I felt distinctly uncomfortable. We said we wanted to eat. "Come, come" said the man, and he opened a door and led us into a room that was so dark we had no idea where we were going. As our eyes adjusted, we could make out booths along the walls, and these were clearly occupied by bodies, which were moving yet making little sound. Out of this room we were led across a vast empty area which I felt might have been a dining room, and into what had very obviously once been a kitchen. A folding table was quickly erected and we were invited to sit. I glanced around, and saw the marks where once upon a time kitchen equipment had been placed.

We cheered up slightly when the menus were produced. They were beautiful leather-bound folders with gold tassels and the name of the hotel embossed in gold writing. We saw we could have 'Boeuf Bourgignon' or Veal Holstein, and Nick was happy to find his favourite foods. We ordered our meals, only to be greeted by derisory laughter as we were informed, "Sorry, only Chinese food – we get from market for you!" We waited in that little room for an hour before paper cartons of Chinese food appeared, but by that time we were all so hungry we forgot about the rats in the drains.

Our rooms were horrific, and miles apart. The thinnest mattresses were on the beds, and one very suspect-looking sheet that didn't fit. There was no soap in the bathroom and only the tiniest towel, the size of a tea towel. The windows were blocked up, and the only light was a fluorescent bar overhead.

I grabbed the bedding from the boys' room, and somehow we settled down to sleep. This was very hard, because at night time the hotel seemed to erupt with noisy chatter and laughter. We were booked in for two nights, but luckily managed to persuade our next hotel in the Cameron Highlands to take us a day early.

All night long I tossed and turned – and itched! The following morning we were all a mass of bites. Richard's back was horrific, and most of my bites were in my head. The children had bites all over them. We left our room just after six am, and had to step over a mass of sleeping bodies in the open area outside our room.

It was quite clear to us what had become of this once grand hotel, but harder to explain to the boys! The man at the desk was really upset we were leaving a day early. Somehow we found our way to the Railway Hotel, where we sat amid faded splendour, eating a decent breakfast.

It was a long and ultimately rather nauseating drive up through thick jungle to the Cameron Highlands. Our little guest house was the most enormous surprise. It was called Foster's Smoke House, and if one shut out the sights and sounds of the Malaysian jungle, one could have sworn one was in England.

Foster's Smokehouse was a timbered cottage set in a garden full of hollyhocks and roses. The air was cool and sweetly scented. The Tudor-style oak door opened to reveal a beamed sitting room, with a roaring fire blazing in an inglenook fireplace. We were welcomed with a tea served on English bone china of hot scones with strawberry jam and cream followed by fruit cake. After the horrors of Ipoh, we thought we had died and gone to heaven.

Our bedrooms had four-poster beds, with pretty wallpaper and chintz curtains. We were told that dinner was to be roast pork with stuffing and crackling!

Colonel Foster was the creator of this enchanting home, and he was a man of singular character. Normally he didn't allow children, but thankfully he made an exception in our case, and was kind enough to compliment us on well-behaved children when we left.

Colonel Foster had served in Malaya during WWII. He fell in love not only with the country, but with a young lady. They married, and together created the Smokehouse. While we were there he also showed us the bigger hotel he was building. Copies of *Country Life* were everywhere, as the Colonel used them to help him furnish his houses. Whenever he saw a piece of furniture or a door or window he liked he cut out the photo and gave it to his craftsmen, who duly recreated what they saw perfectly. The doors opened with Elizabethan catches and all the wrought iron fire implements and so on were faithful copies. The whole experience was a delight.

Next day we decided to take a picnic and go for a walk in the Highlands. Mrs Foster warned us to be careful of the "gorillas". It was not until we had been traipsing up a mountain for an hour that we saw warning signs depicting armed men, and realised she had said "guerrillas"! Richard was ruthless in making us climb to the top. "The view will be wonderful when we get there," he assured us.

Unfortunately it began to rain. I don't know who was more miserable, me or the children. We moaned and grumbled our way to the top and when we finally arrived we saw absolutely nothing, thanks to the heavy rain.

On the way down we kept on losing our footing and

skidding on wet mud as we slid uncontrollably down the mountain. Naturally we were lost, and naturally it was beginning to get dark. I was becoming increasingly nervous. We were all absolutely drenched. When we finally got there the sight of Foster's Smokehouse was never more welcome and soon we were all lying in hot baths while picking several leeches off our bodies! Mrs Foster told us they had been on the point of sending out search parties for us, as this was exactly the area where Jim Thomson disappeared only a few years before.

Next day we decided to stay in the area, as Richard planned to teach his family how to play golf. My husband did at least have a vague knowledge of the game, but the boys and I were complete novices. Little local boys did well out of us. At almost every shot we lost balls in the jungle foliage, and a short time later these balls would be sold back to us by smiling children.

Richard did however have a shining moment. At the last hole, we had to tee off from a very high cliff. The green was far away below us. A group of Japanese players appeared, all beautifully kitted out in proper golfing clothes with masses of clubs. They kindly waited for Richard to show us what to do. In his nervousness, my husband grabbed the first club to hand – a putter. Addressing the ball in the correct manner he took an almighty swipe, and to everyone's total astonishment, the ball serenely soared in the air and landed a mere millimetre away from the hole! The Japanese were lost in admiration and incredulity that a putter was used for such a magnificent shot!

To end our holiday, we had a few days in Bali. I had always wanted to visit Bali, and it didn't disappoint. Our hotel was brilliant and we had our own little cabin with a sea view. Richard and I visited the hotel doctor about our bites, and were both put on antibiotics. It was indeed the perfect place to end such a brilliant trip.

We had to endure a rather terrifying flight back to Sydney on Garuda airlines, but survive we did, and rushed home to find our darling little girl, who had had a whale of a time while we had been away.

★ ★ ★

We had only lived in Sydney for a year when I decided to try my luck at opening a ballet school. However, I had a rival. A teacher of dancing had had the monopoly of running classes in the Eastern Suburbs for many years, and she did not take kindly to someone treading on her toes and usurping her territory. Undeterred however, I determined to see what I could achieve.

By this time I was fortunate enough to have made many friends who had little girls of a suitable age, and they were all prepared to give me a try. I couldn't believe my luck in finding a beautiful hall with a perfect dance floor in Bondi Junction. Added to this, a wonderful woman named Mrs Banes answered my advertisement for a pianist. We hit it off at once, and she became my greatest ally and support, as well as being an excellent pianist.

My one class became three, then five, then two days of five classes each. The children were fantastic, and I don't think I have ever enjoyed teaching more than I did then. I was able to pass on all the wonderful teaching I had received in the past, and I was completely my own mistress. I did not put the children in for exams – they just progressed, and of course I was teaching the Russian method of ballet.

Two days before I had Laura, I very nearly fell when demonstrating some jumps. The audible gasp of horror from the watching mothers brought me to my senses, and I was more careful thereafter.

I produced a small display in the theatre of the school the boys attended. It was a success, and my reputation grew. Only one person wasn't happy – my rival. She spread rumours about me, and often rang me in strange voices to try to trick me into admitting that I was a complete charlatan.

One day I decided to ring her and confront her directly. "Look" I said, "there are hundreds of children in Sydney, and surely you can see that there is plenty of room for us both?"

"You're so right" was the reply, "there is plenty of room for us both because you are so small and insignificant you are not worth even considering!"

I made the dignified choice not to bother with her any more after that.

My next show, two years later, was in a different league. I staged two ballets in a charming little theatre on the edge of Bondi Beach. The first was called "The Ballet of Bondi Beach" and it was set in Victorian times. I could not believe my luck in finding an amazing woman who had the most stunning collection of costumes – many of them original – and took it upon herself to dress my show.

The ballet opened with a scene in the very early hours when two mermaids danced on the empty beach. (Clever these mermaids, to dance on their fishy tails and no legs!) My mermaids were beautiful identical twins called Hilary and Tracy Carpenter. They were stunning little dancers and looked truly out of this world. The mermaids woke the sea nymphs (the babies), who in turn welcomed the sun.

I had such fun creating characters for this ballet, and my 'early morning joggers' in their Victorian bathing costumes and boaters were hysterical. Throughout the day new people appeared, such as nannies with their charges – some good and some not so – and gossipy mothers later joined by the fathers, until the evening came and night descended with the entry of the Spirits of the Night.

The second ballet was about a ballet school that had fallen on hard times. The old ballet mistress (me!) was in despair, but all ended happily when her star pupil returned from a successful tour with a huge cheque to save the school. Little did I know that Madam Rival not only bought a ticket, but also came back stage to talk to my pupils, who had of course been hers, in an effort to entice them back.

When Richard announced after we had lived in Australia for five years that we were to leave and live in Hong Kong, I was devastated. We had fully integrated into Australian life, and had made so many wonderful friends that we were utterly miserable at the thought of uprooting ourselves and starting all over again. I hated to leave my perfect little school. I sold it to another young teacher, but I fear she did nothing with it. I treasure the little notes of farewell I received from my pupils, especially, "Darling Miss Eden, I will always rember you. xxxxx"

I am sure Madam Rival is still whooping with joy at my departure, even though I imagine she is now in the Great Ballet School in the Sky.

★ ★ ★

Richard had been offered a job in Hong Kong with his old agency, Young and Rubicam. We were very ignorant about Hong Kong. All we knew was that it would be completely different from our life in Australia.

"There are no schools in Hong Kong" we were told. "Everybody sends their children to school in the UK."

The thought of my boys being so far away from me filled me with dread. Even so, we listened to what people told us and believed them, and so we made arrangements for Tim and Nick to attend Papplewick School in Ascot. The headmaster had once been a boyfriend of my sister Rose, and he used to be very kind to me when I had been at Heathfield.

In January 1977 Richard stayed behind in Sydney to enjoy the last weeks of party and summer while I took my three little ones to a cold and dark England. The children had no idea what was going on, and probably thought we were just going home for a holiday as usual.

We arrived on the day my brother married for the second time, and no one had time for us. Fritham House was in a state of high activity, and we felt like little Ozzy fishes completely out of water! Laura was so cold and jet-lagged that she slept through the entire reception cocooned in a woollen jumper and hugging a hot-water bottle.

The next week was taken up with buying the new school uniform and frantically sewing on the name tags. I had managed to hire a super New Zealand nanny and she stayed with us in the hotel in London, as by now Victoria Road was no longer my home.

The happy news of my brother's wedding was overshadowed by the growing realization that my sister Ann's second daughter, Emma, was seriously ill. A melanoma was diagnosed, although at that time none of us could foresee the eventual outcome.

The day came when I had to take the boys to their new school. Timothy, the drama king, was in buckets of tears. "When will we see you again, Mummy?" he sobbed. Nicholas bottled it all up and his eyes were dry, but he clenched his fists to show white knuckles as he asked, "Where *is* Hong Kong?"

Laura and I drove to the airport hotel, where we stayed the night. The day before we had celebrated her third birthday with the boys and the rest of the family. It was a month early, but I knew no one in HK to invite to a party for her.

Once we were in the soulless room of the travel hotel, I let my tears fall. My little girl did her best to comfort me by hugging me hard and saying "Don't cwy Mummy, I here." How well she understood.

Richard was very excited to see us. He had had a wonderful few weeks in Sydney, and was now being feted in Hong Kong. He had taken over the apartment, the amah and even the junk of his predecessor. However, as he was working, and also not very good at that sort of thing, he had not unpacked the packing cases, except for some bedding, so I walked into an enormous apartment piled high with boxes. It felt so strange and unlived in.

Richard's plan to take me out to dinner to the Repulse Bay Hotel on my first night was sweet, but unwise. Laura was left in this cavernous, uncosy apartment with a Chinese amah who spoke limited English. She screamed her head off, and we had to leave our wonderful meal to get back to her. It took a while, as our apartment was up on the Peak.

The boxes were unpacked and gradually the excitement of living somewhere so totally new and foreign to us took over. We had the most enormous fun shopping for new furniture, and bought some pieces that still look good, even in Wiltshire.

One day I was kindly invited to lunch with someone I had never met. There I met Lyn Williams, and our conversation went like this:

"How long have you been here?"

"Just three weeks, and you?"

"Also three weeks."

"Have you any children?"

"Two boys in England and a little girl here."

"Oh – how old is she?"

"Just three. How about you?"

"I have a three-year-old daughter too. She's called Laura."

"Oh, so is mine!"

It turned out that we even shared the same wedding date, if a few years apart. This was the beginning of a friendship that is now into its fortieth year.

Our amah was called Ah Ho. She was a 'black and white', which meant she wore black trousers with a white top. Ah Ho had been used to very grand establishments and never hid her disappointment in us. Every evening she would ask me, "Missy likey gin and tonicy?"

"No thank you, Ah Ho," I would reply.

"Oh – then Masser, he likey gin and tonicy?"

"No, he wouldn't either thank you."

Crestfallen, she would retire to the kitchen.

Ah Ho worked six days a week. I was not allowed in the kitchen. Early on I wandered in to prepare Laura's supper, and this misdemeanour was greeted by cries of horror. "Oh no! Missy no come in kitchen. Kitchen Ah Ho's kitchen. No Missy!" So out I went, with my tail between my legs.

Ah Ho was the most phenomenal cook and her Chinese meals were legend. I had to give her a week's warning if we wanted a proper Chinese meal. Her soups were sublime, and I just wish she had taught me a bit more. Communication was difficult between us. "Orla – likey licee lunchee?" translated as "Would Laura like rice for lunch".

Sadly we decided we would be better off with an English-speaking Filipina. However, we could not let Ah Ho lose face, and so with the help of Richard's secretary Ah Ho eventually gave us notice, and we were very sorry to accept.

Our apartment, in a block called Hillcrest, was old fashioned and had very large rooms. However, there were only two bedrooms. Laura's room was huge and had an en suite bathroom. The long passage opened into the vast reception area, which was sitting one side and dining the other. We had a table made for dining, and stupidly had it made to seat twelve, which would prove problematic later. Our bedroom was so big that it had a separate sitting area and two en suite bathrooms, plus a large walk-in cupboard for me and an array of cupboards for Richard. A balcony connected our room to the drawing room, and the views over the South China Sea were stunning.

The kitchen, which had been three rooms, was adequate, and these led on to the Amah's rooms. I was horrified. A dark area leading off the back stairs contained two tiny rooms. The bed was in one room, and the other was used for storage. A chair and table were in the middle, and this part also housed the 'hole in the floor' and a tap. It was archaic, and I was ashamed to think that this was how Ah Ho lived when we were in such splendour. Finally we converted the 'drying room' into a bedroom for the boys when they came on holiday.

Living on the Peak had its drawbacks. For days or weeks at a time one would be encased in cloud. The walls would drip with humidity, and it was easy to stay holed up in one's flat, going nowhere and feeling completely isolated.

Our saviour was our junk. *Double Dutch* by name, this trusty vessel was to entertain us and our friends on many hilarious and memorable occasions. Our skipper – known as a 'Boat Boy' - was called Ah Wah. He was brilliant with the old girl and handled her beautifully, even when we were caught out at sea when signal 3 (the sign of an imminent typhoon) was up. We were all drenched by the tempestuous waves, but we were safe. *Double Dutch* was not grand, like some junks, but she had so much character. Our good friends Annie Pare and Merry Claire Lyle gave me a vibrant plastic parrot on a perch, which became our mascot.

I learned how to ask Ah Wah what the weather was like in Chinese, as stuck in the clouds, I often couldn't tell. Every day he would ring and ask if I wanted to use the junk. One memorable day I was exhausted, and decided to take the junk with Laura, Ella (our Filipina) and their friends. On this occasion Ah Wah also had his brother, Soo Gar (Sugar to us) with him. We sailed to the bay at Lantau, and while I lazed in the sun on the junk the three maids and two boat boys took five children and a dog to the shore. I did nothing – I was Lady Muck. I enjoyed every minute of it, and vowed I would never forget such a decadent and wonderful day.

Thanks to our friendship with Derek Nimmo, we entertained many a famous actor on our little boat as Derek brought plays to HK for limited periods. Huge fun for us, and they all enjoyed the junk experience as well. We also entertained the Seekers, the famous Australian singing group, and well-known politicians such as Peter Rawlinson and Gough Whitlam. Without doubt owning *Double Dutch* was one of the best decisions we ever made.

Once Laura had become used to the Chinese people continually touching her fine blonde hair, she quickly adapted to life in Hong Kong. She made friends with a little girl in our building called Jacquie Bolsover, and this too has turned into a lifelong friendship, with both girls ending up as schoolteachers.

My first months were very hard to bear. I missed my boys dreadfully. At first we corresponded by tapes, but these proved so harrowing as they gulped back their tears and spoke in their Aussie accents that I stopped them, and we relied on letters only. Our American friends in HK thought we were barbarically cruel to send our children away, and Richard and I had many discussions as to what we should do for the best.

The other reason I was so unhappy was the knowledge of what a terrible time my sister was experiencing, as the dreadful truth of her daughter Emma's illness became apparent. Emma was engaged to be married, and was filled with excitement about her future life with her husband-to-be. Ann helped to keep up the appearance that all would be well for her and her other three daughters. Only to me could she let herself go, by writing down the pain and fear she was going through. I would read these letters and cry, desperately praying that the worst outcome would not manifest itself.

Unfortunately it did. Pretty, clever, adored Emma died just days after her 21st birthday. At least her last day was a happy one, planning her wedding with her friends, family and fiancé.

The boys came out to Hong Kong for their first holiday. They wandered around our apartment in amazement, touching all our new furnishings and saying "Is this ours? And this?" They thought HK was brilliantly exciting, and they were also delighted to be reunited with their little sister, as she was with them.

The night before they were due to fly back to UK Tim was in tears, begging me not to put him on the plane, as he knew it was going to crash! The only way I could manage this awful deed was to hand them over as soon as possible and then go to the bar for a brandy!

At the end of the first year, Richard and I made the decision, rightly or wrongly, to take the boys away from Papplewick and school them in Hong Kong. From an educational point of view this was undoubtedly a mistake, but from the point of view of cementing our family, it was perfect.

The ensuing years in Hong Kong were magical. Having been told that Hillcrest was to be pulled down to make way for a high-rise apartment block, we moved to the other side of the island, to Stanley. There we were the first tenants of an apartment that seemed like a small house, with its own front door and an atrium which led up to a large roof terrace. In the complex we shared two tennis courts and a large swimming pool, while we were only minutes from the beach and the famous Stanley market. We were all tremendously happy there, and the boys attended the South Island School while Laura went to the local school by bus every day.

When I first arrived in Hong Kong I made enquiries about ballet schools. I found two, one in Repulse Bay and one in the Helena May Institute. I offered my services, and was hired to teach in both establishments. After a year I decided to branch out on my own, and once again, I had the luck to find the perfect studio in the HK Arts Centre, and a fabulous young Chinese pianist played for my classes. In no time I had built up a small school of about sixty children, and when I held a performance at the end of my first year, someone commented that they hoped no one would bomb the theatre, as every important Tai Pan and businessman was in the audience watching his child!

One day Laura appeared with a fat little puppy in her arms. We quickly ascertained that she was being fattened up for Chinese New Year, so we gave her a home. Ching was a remarkable dog, and so much happened to her in the short time she lived with us that I have written a story about it.

For our first Christmas in HK, we decided to return to Sydney. By this time we were well used to the Australian Christmas and didn't blink an eyelid singing "In The Deep Midwinter" in the searing heat!

Before returning to Hong Kong we had a fascinating and somewhat adventurous holiday in Papua New Guinea. We spent several days on a primitive houseboat on the Sepik River, where we visited tribal communities, some of whom were nomadic and had never seen white people before. We took Laura, although she was only four, and she was the hugest asset. Her hair, as in HK, was fascinating to these people, and they could not resist touching it. We saw and learned so much, and I like to think that these holidays provided alternative education for our children.

All too soon Richard made another change in his career and was wooed back to England. Once again I did not want to leave, as I felt, rightly as it turned out, that we had not been in HK long enough. We made many lifelong friends, especially Bridget and Peter Wrangham who also had a small house on Lantau Island, where we spent many happy weekends.

Once again we had the round of farewell parties, and although I was delighted to be seeing my family again, it was with a really heavy heart that we left the Far East, which had definitely found its way under our skin. Tim, in his adult life, went on to live and work in this part of the world for twenty years.

★ ★ ★

First New York, then Sydney and finally Hong Kong. The farewells began again, and for the third time in our married life I felt we were leaving home and so many delightful friends. I really wanted to stay at least two more years in the Far East, as I had grown to love being in Asia and very much liked the people. We were lucky though, as we were in HK before the handover to the mainland, and life in the colony was still very pro the Westerner. I thought of the occasion I had taken our dear American friend Carpy to dinner at the Mandarin Hotel, only to discover upon our arrival that I had no money, cheque book or credit card, nor any identification. The maitre d', on hearing my predicament, could not have been more charming. He took my name and address and entirely trusted me to pay the following day. He treated me like an honoured customer and we both had a wonderful evening.

Hong Kong was bustling and exciting. My small ballet school was going well, and the children were happy. It was hard to leave. Tim and Nick had already gone back, but Laura came with us on our return to the UK via India. Unfortunately I had managed to contract a severe bout of food poisoning while eating fish in the floating market just before we left. I imported Delhi belly to Delhi! I was monumentally unwell, but had moments of feeling reasonable, so I was able to enjoy some wonderful experiences in India and Kashmir.

The Taj Mahal exceeded all expectations although my lasting memory is of my little girl skipping with her rope all around the monument.

I had always wanted to see Kashmir, as my ballet friend Veronica had filled my imagination with her fascinating stories of holidays there when she lived in India.

We rented a house boat on Lake Nagin, and it was perfect;

small and utterly enchanting. Despite my fragile state, I thought I had never been anywhere more beautiful. Laura loved our guide, Ahmed, and called him Arm Head. She spent hours fishing on the lake with him. The people were charming to us, and I was enchanted by the beauty of the women in their brilliantly-coloured saris and the children — cheeky as all children are — full of smiles and trying to speak English.

We briefly left our houseboat to stay in the mountains at Gulmarg. I awoke to find the fire in my bedroom being made up by a young man who had no soles to his shoes. I wished I had shoes to give him, but could only leave a little money instead. Later that day Laura saw her first snow and had a slide on a tin tray. It is so sad to think it is now not safe to visit Kashmir, and I feel so incredibly lucky to have enjoyed such a special time there.

When we came to leave India I knew we were returning to the next stage of our life back in England.

CHAPTER SEVENTEEN

THE VACANI SCHOOL OF DANCING

It was strange being back in London. It was great to see our friends, but hard to talk to them about our travels to such exotic places as Papua New Guinea or Borneo or Kashmir without appearing to show off. Our old friends had lived their own lives during the past eight years, lives in which we had played no part, and it took a little while to re-establish the friendships we had enjoyed before we left all those years before.

Our priority was finding somewhere to live and settling Laura into school. The latter was not easy, as she was completely thrown and did not enjoy her life in London. I was in the kitchen of our rented house a week after our return when I was aware of Laura standing in the doorway looking at me curiously.

"Why are you in the kitchen, Mummy?" she asked. "Where is Stella?"

"Welcome to the real world, darling" I replied. "From now on you will have to get used to seeing Mummy in the kitchen."

We found a lovely house in Clapham Common and the boys were settled at Marlborough College. To help Laura feel more at home I also found a mongrel puppy, Rosie, as she had been so upset at leaving our Chinese dog, Ching, behind. Rosie became a very important member of our family for the next eighteen years.

After initially teaching drama at an after-school club for Laura's school, Thomas's, I accepted an invitation to lunch which was to change my life for the next twenty-five years.

Laura also spent a couple of years at Lady Eden's School, and before her grandmother died she was able to present her with some flowers at speech day. I was delighted also to have been asked by my brother John to give the speech when Lady Eden's celebrated its 50th anniversary. My mother had not lived to see this occasion, but how proud she would have been.

Thomas's eventually took over Lady Eden's School and a grown-up Laura taught in their schools for many years. Full circle.

It was with a certain amount of curiosity that I accepted Betty Vacani's invitation to lunch at her favourite Italian restaurant opposite the side entrance to Harrods in Knightsbridge in the autumn of 1981. Ever since I could remember, Miss Vacani's dancing school had been situated on the top floor above a bank at 159 Brompton Road. I had attended classes there as a small child, and later as a more advanced student.

My young son Timothy filled me with shame and embarrassment at the end of his first dancing class there. The children were required to hold hands in a line and walk slowly down the hall to bow or curtsey to Miss Vacani. Little Timmy, aged three, looked at the children on either side of him and decided to race down the room, pulling dainty but unsteady toddlers with him. Unfortunately he was unaware that there were two pillars in the centre of the room. The ensuing heap of crying babies had mothers and nannies rushing to the rescue, while I grabbed Timothy and made a hasty exit.

The purpose of the lunch was to introduce me to Mary Stassinopoulos, who, as you would imagine, was Greek. I found Mary to be utterly charming and warmed to her immediately.

I don't know who was more surprised at the question Betty Vacani then asked us. Would the two of us like to buy her school?

With a good deal of understanding, Betty had decided that with a young family I would not be in a position to run the whole school on my own. However, I did have a name that was known in London and this would undoubtedly help. Mary's name was not well known at this time, but she was highly trained in the Cecchetti method of ballet, whereas I had been Russian trained. It was clever of Betty to have thought of us, as in many respects we made an unlikely pair.

Mary had trained in Athens and Switzerland, and until she met BV she had never taught. Betty sent her out to one of the schools, and in no time it was discovered that Mary was an extremely gifted teacher.

Mary and I liked each other instantly. Betty was a tough negotiator, but we eventually arrived at a happy solution and at the start of the spring term in 1982 we found ourselves the new owners of the Vacani School of Dancing.

There was only one drawback, and that was the fact that the lease on the premises was due to expire. "If I was any younger I would just get on my bike and find somewhere else" said Betty. Mary and I nodded, unknowingly. The search for new premises was to dominate our lives for the next three years.

It was decided I would teach the 2-11 year olds. I had never taught children younger than five and doubted a two-year-old could do anything. How wrong I was. I came to adore this age group, and was constantly amazed at how much a child this young can absorb, understand and enjoy. As time wore on I became quite the expert, and trained many of our teachers, who are still using my methods wherever they are now teaching.

As Mary was Cecchetti trained (as opposed to RAD or Russian) she taught the older pupils. The division worked perfectly, and I soon became Cecchetti enough to enter my pupils for their exams.

We had some teething problems in our first year. Some older staff members who weren't sure about these newcomers created a little difficulty. Betty V, to show we had her support, would come and watch the classes, and then comment to us and any parents who were watching, "We don't normally do it like that". Gritting our teeth, Mary and I presented a united front and banned all parents from watching the classes every week (except the baby classes) and instead presented them with a show class at the end of the term, demonstrating the progress that had been made. We were unpopular for a while, but it worked and soon became accepted.

Try as we might, we could not find alternative premises. To house a ballet school you need a large hall/studio, plus adequate changing areas and an office. It must not be in a residential area, and parking should be accessible. Added to this, the rent has to be affordable. However, from £3,000 p.a. we were looking at £13,000, £25,000 and eventually £30,000.

When our lease expired, we had nowhere to go. We rented a hall here and another there. Our wonderful bursar and ultimately our Associate Director, Mrs Lee Williams, tried to run the school from her flat. Unfortunately BT didn't transfer the line, and everyone thought we had closed. Pupils left in their droves. Mary and I worked tirelessly for no money, just as long as we could pay our staff. We had some excellent teachers who stayed the course with us, and gradually we built up classes in the halls we had hired in other parts of London. In 1986 I decided to start a keep-fit class, as they were becoming all the rage. In Hong Kong I gave a class which I had based on ballet exercises to jazzy music, and I decided to try this while still in Brompton Road. I also attended classes myself to learn new methods. The classes proved a success, with at least fifteen ladies attending on a regular basis.

One memorable day, about ten minutes before the class was due to begin, a bearded, duffle-coated man in his late thirties walked into the studio. He carried a Harrods plastic bag, and asked me if he could join the keep-fit class. He refused to be put off, so I asked the ladies, who said they didn't mind, as they were used to a couple of men who did ballet with us.

The class started with no sign of Mr Duffle Coat, who had to change in the WC. Suddenly the door bust open, and out came this apparition, dressed in the palest, sheerest pink tights and pale pink leotard. Not much was left to the imagination! He put himself in the front row and joined in the exercise. I thought the ladies would have a collective apoplectic fit!

I decided to carry on as if it was the most normal thing in the world to have a bearded man dressed in the palest of pink ballet clothes cavorting in front of me. Somehow we got through the class, and when he eventually reappeared, I tried as tactfully as possible to say he should not come again. I don't think he minded too much. He had had his fun – and we certainly had something to talk about!

Our lease was thankfully extended for one more year, but still we had found no replacement. We looked in Kensington, Chelsea, Victoria, Pimlico, Bayswater, Notting Hill, Fulham, Earl's Court and West Kensington. You name it, we went there. Then one day an agent showed us an enormous building in South Kensington which had been empty for some time. Originally a church, it had then become the HQ for a circus company. The top floor was one enormous area with vaulted ceilings. The building and area were perfect, if only… if only we had the money and the backing.

I immediately saw the potential of realising my dream of creating a venue where girls, boys and adults could all come at the same time, somewhere we could teach ballet, modern, jazz, tap and drama, gym and a range of adult classes. It was so frustrating to have the idea, to find the premises, but to have no money.

Mary and I admitted defeat, and then we heard that Debbie Moore of Pineapple Dance Studios had bought the building. "Nothing ventured, nothing gained", I said to myself, so I wrote to Debbie and asked her if she would consider us as permanent tenants. A few meetings later, all was agreed. This was the beginning of a happy association that lasted many years. The building had five studios in all, and a coffee shop. As time went by, we used three studios at the same time, three days each week. Our teachers also visited several schools both in and out of London, and for a brief period we went international, with classes in Paris! I was so excited to have finally found permanent premises, and wrote at once to inform our Patron, HM Queen Elizabeth the Queen Mother. A few days later a large and beautiful portrait of Queen Elizabeth the Queen Mother was delivered to us, duly signed by her and dated 1984.

Harrington Road was the perfect venue, and despite some problems, the pupils kept pouring in. We also kept several of the halls in other areas going, as we had built up a local clientele. With the help of Lee Williams, Val Birrell and Nancy Price in the office, our numbers eventually increased to over 600 pupils a week at Harrington Road alone.

In 1986 I decided to start a branch in Clapham close to where we lived. I had five pupils in three classes on the first day, and the new pianist left in disgust. Eventually this branch grew to over 400. The pianist should have stayed.

The classes in Broomwood Hall, Clapham, became my favourite. We had five afternoons weekly at this branch, and I just loved teaching there. I worked out that at this time I taught twenty-two classes per week, walked my dog twice a day and played tennis on Fridays, as well as running a home with three children. I think I was quite fit!

Our reputation was growing, not only for the fun classes we gave, but also for the excellent exam results we obtained. In the ensuing years several of our pupils were accepted at vocational schools such as the Royal Ballet School, the Arts Educational School and Elmhurst. A satisfying number of Mary's pupils continued to make a career in dance. Some of my pupils switched to acting, including Sienna Miller and Olivia Grant. Miss Stass (as she came to be known) was often invited to see her ex-pupils dancing in the various companies they had joined. My partner had by this time qualified as an Examiner and Licentiate of the Cecchetti Society.

We also produced large performances every other year. These were held in West End theatres in aid of charity. Our first one in November 1985 was attended, just, by Princess Margaret. She insisted on arriving during the interval and leaving before the end. The timing had to be exact, and it was somewhat nerve-racking. Our good friend David Jacobs compered this event. My childhood friend Anna Massey was our Guest of Honour in 1987.

Our biggest triumph was producing the full-length ballet of *The Nutcracker* TWICE on the same day, with different casts but the same costumes! A useful side effect of these shows was how much weight I lost! We often had over one hundred children in a show.

Apart from major events we held week-long holiday clubs which were open to boys and girls alike. We offered courses in Drama, Tap, Modern and Ballroom Dancing. In the non-matinee years we presented fashion shows. These shows were charming and much easier for us. The clothes were provided, and we created simple dances to show them off, with titles like *The Seaside, A Party, A Winter's Day* and so forth. We held a successful show at the Savoy Hotel, where we raised thousands of pounds for a leukaemia charity. The children looked enchanting, helped by the expertise of Malcolm and Karen Twist doing their hair and make-up.

Unfortunately one of these shows ended in near disaster. We were showing a collection of clothes in a London hotel in aid of the Blind Society. Our Guest of Honour was Queen Anne Marie of Greece, as her daughter was a pupil. Also in our cast was little Elizabeth Jagger. I had promised her parents not to publicise this fact, but Elizabeth was adorable and I knew would be good. Jerry Hall agreed to draw the raffle.

I could not believe my eyes when I arrived at the hotel to find it totally swamped with paparazzi. These 'gentlemen' of the press barged into the ballroom and grabbed the front row seats from parents who had paid for them, and several of them also pushed into the room where the children were changing. No amount of begging, pleading, ordering, cajoling or threatening would move them. I was close to tears. When Elizabeth appeared they flashed their cameras in her face and then disappeared. I was mortified.

At Vacani we had taught several children of famous people. Members of our Royal Family, and those from abroad, sent their children to us. Well-known people from the theatrical and business world send us their children as well. We made it a point never to publicise this fact. Regrettably on this occasion, Mick Jagger and Jerry Hall blamed us entirely and wouldn't listen to my protestations. They took their daughter away. Later I discovered it had been the charity that had notified the press, as they thought they would get more publicity that way. Ah well!

Because Miss Vacani and her partner Miss Hanes had taught the Queen and Princess Margaret when they were children, as well as Prince Charles and Princess Anne, HRH Queen Elizabeth the Queen Mother very delightfully remained our Patron when we took over the school. We exchanged many letters over the years, and at a Buckingham Palace garden party we were invited to meet her. We were stunned by Her Majesty commenting knowledgeably on our wonderful pianists, our problem floors and our good exam results! What a remarkable person she was. We were thrilled to be able to take part in the two huge parades for her 90th and 100th birthday celebrations, and she and Prince Charles waved enthusiastically as we passed by.

Vacani teachers visited several schools both in and out of

London on a weekly basis. The size of our staff grew, as in London we held classes in Swiss Cottage, Bayswater, Chelsea, Fulham, Clapham, East Sheen and Richmond, as well as Harrington Road.

The outside branches of Vacani were growing so fast, and we had such excellent teachers in charge of them, that we used to hold matinee performances just for them. On one of these occasions Mary and I stood in the wings, watching a charming little ballet from the East Sheen branch. We were so pleased with the children and their teacher that we couldn't resist giving ourselves a little hug of satisfaction.

Betty Vacani sadly died a few years after we had taken over, but not before we were able to give her a special birthday surprise in the form of a little ballet. We first performed this at a garden party, but at her request we repeated it at 'my' old theatre, the Duke of York's in the West End.

Betty was on the stage and the whole ballet was for her. The postman arrived with a sack of cards, all created by the children for her, and then she was given presents, each of which was accompanied by a dance. Finally there was a party, and she adored the 'wobbly jellies' and a terrific tap dance by the 'Smarties'. The high point was a huge cake which somehow managed to hide all the children who burst out of it to sing to her! I like to think she felt she had left her school in safe hands and had no regrets when she died.

My mother was extremely proud of the success Mary and I were having with Vacani. She loved to hear all my stories about the school and the children. It had been her wish that I would eventually take over the running of Lady Eden's School, and she always referred to it as "our school" with this in mind. Dear Helen Wakeford had promised to keep the seat warm for me. Unfortunately, this was not to be. In the mind of my mother, owning and running Vacani was the next best thing. Betty and Mummy had been friends for many years.

My mother really wanted to see one of our shows, so I arranged for her to be driven to London to see a matinee we held at the Queen Elizabeth Hall on the South Bank. However Mummy awoke in her cottage in the New Forest to thick snow, and the approach to her house was impassable by car. Only a tractor towing a trailer could negotiate this drive. Despite her age and all her afflictions after her stroke, nothing was going to stop my mother from coming. So, not caring how she looked, she coped with the trailer until she was able to transfer to the comfort of the car.

It gave me such pleasure to be able to show her the ballet school Mary and I had created. Mummy adored the performance, especially the hornpipe dance which I had choreographed at her request.

In June 1990 I was preparing to celebrate my fiftieth birthday, but a week earlier Mummy had another severe stroke. We knew we were looking at the end, but still we hoped. On 14th June Richard gave me a wonderful party. The following morning, the date of my sister Rose's birthday, our darling mother died.

For all her annoyances and strange habits, she was indeed a wonderful mother and a terrific personality. Her death left a huge gap in our lives and to this day we talk about her and remember her. No doubt if she had not had her strokes she would have lived many more years. At the time of writing her youngest sister, Phil, is about to celebrate her 102nd birthday. They had strong hearts in that family.

The school continued happily for the next few years until suddenly we received a major blow. Pineapple had sold the building, and the new owners wanted us out. Despite pleas and petitions, with even a sweet letter from the Queen Mother hoping we would not have to move, we had to leave our perfect premises and relocate, at incredibly short notice. We found a hall opposite Victoria Coach station, but we managed to lose two thirds of our pupils in doing so as most people seemed to think we had moved just to inconvenience them.

It took another three years, but eventually numbers were well up again. We felt sure we were safe there, but once again we had to leave. We felt particularly hurt as the place had been in a bad state when we had arrived and in three years we had turned it into a thriving building. On this occasion we were not so lucky. We found a good hall in Pimlico, but as we were not the sole occupiers the times we could teach were restricted. It was beginning to feel like struggling uphill and then constantly sliding back again.

After the Queen Mother died in 2002, the ballerina Bryony Brind became our patron. We still produced shows and held exams, with impressive results. Our adult classes were growing in popularity and all our other branches were still doing well. However, overall our numbers were down from the heady days when we had taught 1,300 children a week.

By then, after thirty-five years of teaching, I was beginning to feel a little tired. Our stalwart bursar and friend Lee Williams was beginning to feel the same. I decided to retire from teaching and concentrate on running the classes we held at the Hurlingham Club in Fulham. I did this for another five years, until my husband also retired. Then, with a heavy heart, Mary and I decided that the time had come to try and sell the whole school. We divided up the branches and were delighted to be able to sell all but one, with Bayswater and Clapham retaining the Vacani name. These are run by Kezia Mitchell and Angelina Spurrier, both loyal Vacani teachers. Mary was able to continue teaching at Pimlico when she was available and Gaie Loftie continued to teach the Vacani method for years to great acclaim.

Vacani had been my life for so many years. My children used to dread going anywhere with me, as without fail, someone would say "Hello, Miss Eden!" France, Italy, USA, Singapore – I constantly met present and past pupils. I did think I was safe on a small plane in South Africa during term time, but no – "Hello Miss Eden!" came the call, and there was Cherie Lunghi, the actress, with her daughter.

To this day I keep meeting either ex-pupils or their parents who are good enough to thank me for the years of enjoyment I gave them, either in practice or watching. Some children I knew would never become dancers, but I hope I taught them some grace, and some enjoyment of dance and appreciation of music. I would often peep from behind the curtains during our performances to watch the faces of parents and grandparents. The expressions of total enjoyment, amusement and pride on their faces were all the reward I needed.

We were lucky over the years to have had such incredibly talented pianists accompanying our classes. It was always so important to us, and they too have become part of the Vacani legend: Mr Keith, Mr Charles, Stephen, Sujeeva and dear Mrs Davies, who played until she was 95. These are only a few of the inspirational pianists who used to help make the classes so enjoyable for everyone.

Mary and I worked very well together, and we both admired talents in each other. Several of our students qualified as teachers themselves, and some are now running their own schools.

What fun it all was, even the ups and the downs we had to

endure. We had our dramas, and we had our moments of hilarity. I believe that both Mary and I can look back and remember that first time we met with Betty Vacani, and say to ourselves, in the words (almost) of a well-known entertainer, "Haven't we done well?"

Apart from our own enjoyment and satisfaction in teaching, we had the gratification of knowing that we had raised approximately £100,000 for the various charities we supported. Now, in the peace of the Wiltshire countryside, I can enjoy reading our old programmes and the letters from parents and pupils I have kept. These, along with a mass of photographs, help me to recall the literally hundreds of children who came to Miss Eden and Miss Stass at the Vacani School of Dancing.